CHRISTIAN
BEGINNINGS
AND THE
DEAD SEA
SCROLLS

ACADIA STUDIES IN BIBLE AND THEOLOGY

Craig A. Evans and Lee Martin McDonald, General Editors

The last two decades have witnessed dramatic developments in biblical and theological study. Full-time academics can scarcely keep up with fresh discoveries, recently published primary texts, ongoing archaeological work, new exegetical proposals, experiments in methods and hermeneutics, and innovative theological syntheses. For students and nonspecialists, these developments are confusing and daunting. What has been needed is a series of succinct studies that assess these issues and present their findings in a way that students, pastors, laity, and nonspecialists will find accessible and rewarding. Acadia Studies in Bible and Theology, sponsored by Acadia Divinity College in Wolfville, Nova Scotia, and in conjunction with the college's Hayward Lectureship, constitutes such a series.

The Hayward Lectureship has brought to Acadia many distinguished scholars of Bible and theology, such as Sir Robin Barbour, John Bright, Leander Keck, Helmut Koester, Richard Longenecker, Martin Marty, Jaroslav Pelikan, Ian Rennie, James Sanders, and Eduard Schweizer. The Acadia Studies in Bible and Theology series reflects this rich heritage.

These studies are designed to guide readers through the ever more complicated maze of critical, interpretive, and theological discussion taking place today. But these studies are not introductory in nature; nor are they mere surveys. Authored by leading authorities in the field, the Acadia Studies in Bible and Theology series offers critical assessments of the major issues that the church faces in the twenty-first century. Readers will gain the requisite orientation and fresh understanding of the important issues that will enable them to take part meaningfully in discussion and debate.

Previously published volumes:

I. Howard Marshall, *Beyond the Bible: Moving from Scripture to Theology*

James D. G. Dunn, *A New Perspective on Jesus: What the Quest for the Historical Jesus Missed*

John G. Stackhouse, Jr., *Finally Feminist: A Pragmatic Christian Understanding of Gender*

CHRISTIAN
BEGINNINGS
AND THE
DEAD SEA
SCROLLS

EDITED BY
JOHN J. COLLINS
AND CRAIG A. EVANS

Baker Academic
Grand Rapids, Michigan

©2006 by John J. Collins and Craig A. Evans

Published by Baker Academic
a division of Baker Publishing Group
P.O. Box 6287, Grand Rapids, MI 49516-6287
www.bakeracademic.com

Printed in the United States of America

Library of Congress Cataloging-in-Publication Data
Christian beginnings and the Dead Sea scrolls / edited by John J. Collins
    and Craig A. Evans.
        p.   cm. — (Acadia studies in Bible and theology)
    Includes bibliographical references and indexes.
    ISBN 10: 0-8010-2837-X (pbk.)
    ISBN 978-0-8010-2837-3 (pbk.)
    1. Christianity—Origin. 2. Dead Sea scrolls. 3. Church history—Primi-
tive and early church, ca. 30–600. 4. Judaism (Christian theology)—
History. I. Collins, John Joseph, 1946– II. Evans, Craig A. III. Series.
BR129.C42 2006
270.1—dc22   2006013321

Contents

CONTRIBUTORS

Martin G. Abegg Jr. (Ph.D., Hebrew Union College) is Ben Zion Wacholder Professor of Dead Sea Scrolls Studies at Trinity Western University in British Columbia. He is also director of the Dead Sea Scrolls Institute and author and translator of a number of books.

John J. Collins (Ph.D., Harvard University) is Holmes Professor of Old Testament Criticism and Interpretation at Yale Divinity School. He has served as editor of the *Journal of Biblical Literature* and has authored many books, including *The Scepter and the Star* (Doubleday) and *Daniel* in the acclaimed Hermeneia Commentary (Fortress).

Craig A. Evans (Ph.D., Claremont Graduate University) is Payzant Distinguished Professor of New Testament at Acadia Divinity College in Nova Scotia. He has served as editor of the *Bulletin for Biblical Research* and has authored many books, including *Jesus and His Contemporaries* (Brill) and *Mark* in the Word Biblical Commentary (Nelson).

Barry D. Smith (Ph.D., McMaster University) is associate professor of philosophy and religious studies at Atlantic Baptist University in New Brunswick. He has authored *Jesus' Last Passover Meal* (Mellen) and *Paul's Seven Explanations of the Suffering of the Righteous* (Lang).

Jonathan R. Wilson (Ph.D., Duke University) is Pioneer McDonald Professor of Theology at Carey Theological College in British Columbia. He has authored many books, including *Living Faithfully in a Fragmented World* (Trinity) and *God So Loved the World* (Baker).

R. Glenn Wooden (Ph.D., University of St. Andrews) is associate professor of Old Testament at Acadia Divinity College in Nova Scotia. He is co-editor of *"You Will Be My Witnesses": Essays in Honour of Allison Trites* (Mercer University Press) and is writing *Daniel* in the New International Commentary on the Old Testament (Eerdmans).

PREFACE

The Dead Sea Scrolls, discovered more than half a century ago at Qumran, on the northeast coast of the Dead Sea, have proved to be the most important modern discovery related to biblical literature, Judaism of late antiquity, and nascent Christianity. Some nine hundred scrolls have been recovered. The exact number is uncertain, due to the fragmentary condition of so many.[1] More than two hundred scrolls are copies of Jewish Scripture, or what Christians call the Old Testament, and the Old Testament Apocrypha, or Deuterocanonical books. A great number of the scrolls are sectarian, probably produced by or related in some way to the group identified by ancient writers as Essenes. These writings include commentaries (or pesharim) on Scripture, rules and regulations (such as 1QS and related documents), hymns, calendars, and writings concerned with the final struggle against and victory over evil (as seen in the *War Scroll* and related documents).[2]

The scrolls have made an important contribution to our understanding of the development of the text and canon of Scrip-

1. Qumran's Cave 4 yielded the greatest number of scrolls, with some six hundred in all.

2. For a scholarly assessment of the scrolls, see P. W. Flint and J. C. VanderKam, eds., *The Dead Sea Scrolls after Fifty Years: A Comprehensive Assessment* (2 vols.; Leiden: Brill, 1998–99). For a more popular treatment, see J. C. VanderKam and P. W. Flint, *The Meaning of the Dead Sea Scrolls: Their Significance for Understanding the Bible, Judaism, Jesus, and Christianity* (San Francisco: HarperCollins, 2002).

ture. Almost all of the books that make up the Jewish Bible are represented.[3] The Hebrew text of many scrolls matches the Hebrew of what eventually became known as the Masoretic Text. The Samaritan Hebrew text is attested, as well as a Hebrew text that corresponds to the Old Greek, or Septuagint. Indeed, we may also have a fourth Hebrew text type, unknown to us prior to the discovery of the scrolls.

Multiple copies of Tobit, Sirach, *1 Enoch*, and *Jubilees* suggest that these writings may well have been thought of as Scripture at Qumran. At the very least, the evidence of Qumran indicates that the canon of Scripture, as later defined by the rabbis, had not yet been settled.[4]

Some of the Bible scrolls clear up textual problems. The story of King Nahash of the Ammonites seems incomplete, as preserved in 1 Samuel 10:27–11:1. Josephus apparently knew more of the story (cf. *Antiquities* 6.68–71). The discovery of 4QSamuel[a] confirms that some of the narrative is missing from the Masoretic tradition. The fuller version of the story is now restored (compare the RSV and the NRSV of 1 Sam. 10:27). There is also a problem with Psalm 145, an acrostic psalm in which each verse begins with the succeeding letter of the Hebrew alphabet, from *aleph* (א) to *taw* (ת). Since the Masoretic Text does not have a verse beginning with *nûn* (נ), textual critics assumed that a colon between verse 13 and verse 14, beginning with the letter *nûn*, had been in the original version of the psalm. The Greek version has the corresponding verse: "Faithful is the Lord in his words." The Greek word for "faithful" (*pistos*) readily translates into a Hebrew equivalent beginning with *nûn* (*ne'ĕmān*). This scholarly assumption was confirmed by the scrolls. 11QPsalms[a]

---

3. No fragment of Esther has been found. Nothing of Nehemiah has been found either, but the presence of Ezra, which in antiquity was usually combined with Nehemiah, suggests that the latter may also have been among the Bible scrolls.

4. For a convenient collection of the Bible scrolls, presented in English and more or less in canonical order, see M. G. Abegg Jr., P. W. Flint, and E. Ulrich, *The Dead Sea Scrolls Bible: The Oldest Known Bible Translated for the First Time into English* (San Francisco: HarperCollins, 1999). One should also consult L. M. McDonald and J. A. Sanders, eds., *The Canon Debate* (Peabody, MA: Hendrickson, 2002). Especially relevant to the present discussion is the chapter by J. C. VanderKam: "Questions of Canon Viewed through the Dead Sea Scrolls" (91–109).

preserves the missing verse, reading only slightly differently from the Greek: "Faithful is God in his words." Finally, according to 1 Samuel 17:4, the giant Goliath was six cubits in height, or about 9'9". This seems an impossible size. The Greek reads four cubits, or about 6'6". This is still tall, especially for antiquity, but it is anatomically possible. 4QSamuel[a] agrees with the Greek, showing that the more plausible reading was known to the Hebrew tradition as well. Other examples like this could be cited, further underscoring the important contribution that the Dead Sea Scrolls have made to our understanding of the development and preservation of the text of Scripture.

The scrolls have also made important contributions to our knowledge in areas of doctrine, especially pertaining to law and eschatological expectations. The scrolls help bridge the gap between the laws of Moses, expressed in the Pentateuch, and the later rabbinic laws that eventually came to expression in the Mishnah, Tosefta, Talmud, and midrashim. The scrolls, moreover, provide a helpful context in which we can better understand the messianic enthusiasm of first- and second-century revolutionaries like Theudas, Simon bar Gioras, or Simon ben Kosiba (popularly known as Bar Kokhba), on the one hand, and the Christology that developed in the movement that Jesus of Nazareth initiated, on the other. The scrolls were not written by rabbis or Christians, but the scrolls preserve traditions that we now recognize were at many points the antecedents of what later emerged as rabbinic Judaism and Christianity.

The papers that make up the present volume speak to these issues. The essays by John Collins and Craig Evans address Jewish messianism and hopes of national restoration.

Collins addresses two recent books, *The First Messiah* by Michael Wise and *The Messiah before Jesus* by Israel Knohl, each of which argues that the Christian idea of a suffering messiah is anticipated in the scrolls. Wise argues that the Teacher of Righteousness models himself on the Suffering Servant of Isaiah 40–55, in the *Hodayot*, or *Thanksgiving Hymns*, especially in the hymns that he is often thought to have composed. A good case can be made that the teacher modeled himself on the servant, but it is not likely that he was regarded as a messiah. The scrolls always refer to the messiahs (of Aaron and Israel) as figures who were still to come in the future. Knohl bases his argument on a fragmentary but fascinating text in which the speaker claims to have a throne in heaven and also applies to himself language associated with the Suffering Servant. This text offers an intriguing parallel to early Christianity. It is uncertain whether the speaker is a historical person or an eschatological messiah. Knohl's attempt to identify him as an Essene teacher around the turn of the era is not persuasive. Neither is there any evidence that the figure in question was thought to die and rise again. The parallel with Christian beliefs about Jesus is potentially important, but only partial.

Evans investigates three typologies—wilderness, baptism, and the number twelve. All three grow out of Scripture, and all three informed various Jewish restoration movements in late antiquity. These typologies not only link the founders of the Christian movement (John, Jesus, and Paul) but are paralleled in some respects in the Dead Sea Scrolls. No direct lines of contact between the founders of the Christian movement and the scrolls are suggested, but it is argued that the theology and teaching of the former cannot be adequately understood without careful consideration of the latter.

The essays by Martin Abegg and Barry Smith speak to issues of law and obedience, as clarified by the scrolls. Both make important contributions to our understanding of the religious context in which early Christian theology emerged.

Abegg addresses what today is regarded as the most important question in the study of Paul. Just how did the apostle understand "works of the law" in relation to justification, and in what way does 4QMMT, a letter from Qumran in which the Hebrew equivalent of this phrase appears, relate to Paul? Abegg returns to this lively debate, arguing that the author of 4QMMT is speaking of works of law that one must do to maintain covenant status, not to gain entry into the covenant.

Smith approaches the topic from a different angle. His concerns are pertinent for Pauline studies (e.g., as in Rom. 8), but he limits himself primarily to the data of the scrolls themselves. He reviews the language and conceptuality of the phrase "spirit of holiness" and how this power makes obedience in the present time possible and how it will empower the faithful more fully in the future. Smith rightly recognizes that these Qumran texts can shed light on the meaning and role of the Holy Spirit in the New Testament.

The studies by Glenn Wooden and Jonathan Wilson explore questions of hermeneutics and theology.

Wooden explores the intriguing topic of inspired interpretation, in both the Dead Sea Scrolls and in the writings of the New Testament. The Holy Spirit provides a hermeneutical plus, enabling the interpreter to find application and truth not always obvious to others. The belief in divinely aided interpretation of Scripture was widely held in some circles, and apart from this belief we cannot fully appreciate what is often encountered in the New Testament.

Wilson considers recent work by New Testament scholars and theologians on apocalyptic theology, especially in the writings of Paul, as a model for interdisciplinary collaboration. He asks whether the Dead Sea Scrolls can provide us with another apocalyptic vision on which we could reflect and whether apocalyptic theology is necessarily sectarian. In a brief response to Wilson's essay, John Collins argues that the scrolls do indeed provide another apocalyptic vision and that they provide a cautionary lesson for Christian theology. A theology based on apocalyptic assertion lends itself to sectarianism, and such a theology is not likely to be persuasive to many people for long.

The studies gathered in this small volume touch on some of the major issues that the Dead Sea Scrolls have raised for the study of early Christianity. The authors of these studies have benefited from the passage of time, since the exciting days of the publication of the remaining unpublished scrolls in 1991. The authors have pondered their subjects in the light of fifteen years or so of discussion and debate that ensued and now present to general readers the results of their study and reflections. In so doing, they contribute to a discussion and debate that will undoubtedly occupy scholars for many years to come.

The present collection of studies was occasioned by a special edition of the Hayward Lectures, sponsored by Acadia Divinity College. These lectures were given in March 2004. The editors thank Dr. Lee Martin McDonald, president of the seminary; the presenters, whose papers, in revised form, appear in this volume; and the Rev. John E. Boyd and the late Dr. Byron W. Fenwick, who presided over the morning and afternoon sessions. Byron is deeply missed.

The editors also thank the Social Sciences and Humanities Research Council of Canada and Baker Academic for financial support. A word of thanks is also owed to Danny Zacharias for preparing the indexes.

John J. Collins
Yale Divinity School

Craig A. Evans
Acadia Divinity College

1

A MESSIAH BEFORE JESUS?

John J. Collins

The Dead Sea Scrolls are the main corpus of primary documents from ancient Judea around the turn of the era. The era in question was a tumultuous one. Judea was under Roman rule and would eventually erupt in a disastrous revolt, leading to the destruction of Jerusalem and its temple. In the century leading up to the revolt, the unrest spawned a series of "bandits, prophets, and messiahs," promising deliverance of one sort or another to an oppressed people.[1] Only one of these would have a lasting impact on history, Jesus of Nazareth, who was executed in Jerusalem under Pontius Pilate around 30 CE. Part of the fascination of the scrolls for the general public has always lain in the possibility that they might throw some light on the career of Jesus or on the beginnings of Christianity. One of the most controversial issues in this regard has been the intermittent

1. R. A. Horsley and J. S. Hanson, *Bandits, Prophets, and Messiahs: Popular Movements in the Time of Jesus* (Minneapolis: Winston, 1985). See also John J. Collins, *The Scepter and the Star: The Messiahs of the Dead Sea Scrolls and Other Ancient Literature* (New York: Doubleday, 1995), 195–214.

claim that the scrolls, or more specifically the figure known as the Teacher of Righteousness, anticipated Jesus in some significant way. This issue was especially controversial in the 1950s, during the early years of research on the scrolls. It received renewed impetus in the early 1990s when the entire corpus of the scrolls became generally available for the first time. And recently it has been brought to the fore again in two books, one by a Christian scholar, Michael Wise's *First Messiah*, and the other by a Jewish scholar, Israel Knohl's *Messiah before Jesus*.[2]

The Older Debate

Already in 1950, a mere three years after the first discoveries of scrolls near the Dead Sea, André Dupont-Sommer of the Sorbonne delivered a public lecture in which he argued that the Teacher of Righteousness, the revered leader of the sect described in the scrolls, was held to be a messiah and was persecuted, tortured, and put to death. In short, he was in many ways "the exact prototype of Jesus."[3] The lecture caused an uproar. Dupont-Sommer qualified and defended his views in several publications over the following decade. He insisted that he had never dreamt of denying either the existence or the originality of Jesus of Nazareth.[4] In part, his argument rested on a controversial reading of the pesher on Habakkuk, especially the key passage found in column 11:

> Woe to him who causes his neighbour to drink, who pours out his fury (upon him) till he is drunk, that they may gaze on their feasts!
> The explanation of this concerns the Wicked Priest who persecuted the Teacher of Righteousness, swallowing him up in the anger of his fury in his place of exile. But at the time of the feast

2. Michael Wise, *The First Messiah: Investigating the Savior before Jesus* (San Francisco: Harper, 1999); and Israel Knohl, *The Messiah before Jesus: The Suffering Servant of the Dead Sea Scrolls* (Berkeley: University of California Press, 2000).

3. See Michael Baigent and Richard Leigh, *The Dead Sea Scrolls Deception* (London: Jonathan Cape, 1991), 44. The lecture was reported in *Le Monde*, May 28–29, 1950, 4.

4. A. Dupont-Sommer, *The Essene Writings from Qumran* (trans. G. Vermes; repr. Gloucester, MA: Smith, 1973), 373.

of rest of the Day of Atonement he appeared before them to swallow them up and to cause them to stumble on the Day of Fasting, their Sabbath of rest.[5]

Dupont-Sommer insisted that the verb *bāla'*, translated "swallow" in this passage, means "to kill." Other commentators allow for a less fatal meaning. He also insisted that the Teacher of Righteousness, after his death, "swallowed" his adversaries. Virtually all other commentators agree, however, that the reference is to the Wicked Priest, who disrupted the sectarian observance of the Day of Atonement. This part of Dupont-Sommer's argument has found no followers in recent times. His interpretation of the teacher, however, also drew on the *Hodayot*, which contain several allusions to passages in the book of Isaiah that are known to modern scholars as the Servant Songs. Dupont-Sommer wrote: "Defining the mission of Jesus as prophet and saviour, the primitive Christian Church explicitly applied these Songs of the Servant of the Lord to him; about a century earlier, the Teacher of Righteousness applied them to himself."[6] The teacher, then, anticipated Jesus, and likewise, we might say, Dupont-Sommer anticipated the argument of Michael Wise.[7]

The controversy in the 1950s went beyond the scholarly debate about the writings of Dupont-Sommer. Edmund Wilson, a literary critic and intellectual with no knowledge of ancient Judaism, found Dupont-Sommer's ideas attractive and brought them to the attention of a wider public. "If," he wrote, "we look now at Jesus in the perspective supplied by the scrolls, we can trace a new continuity and, at last, get some sense of the drama that culminated in Christianity. . . . The monastery [of Qumran] . . . is perhaps, more than Bethlehem or Nazareth,

5. Ibid., 266.
6. Ibid., 361.
7. For early critiques of Dupont-Sommer, see William H. Brownlee, "The Servant of the Lord in the Qumran Scrolls," *Bulletin of the American Schools of Oriental Research* 132 (1953): 8–15; 133 (1954): 33–38; Jean Carmignac, "Les citations de l'Ancien Testament, et specialement des poèmes du Serviteur, dans les hymnes de Qumran," *Revue de Qumran* 2 (1959–60): 357–94; and Gert Jeremias, *Der Lehrer der Gerechtigkeit* (Göttingen: Vandenhoeck & Ruprecht, 1963), 302–4.

the cradle of Christianity."[8] Wilson also suggested that the scholars working on the scrolls were "somewhat inhibited in dealing with such questions as these by their various religious commitments."[9] Then in 1956 John Allegro, a member of the official team of scholars editing the scrolls, gave a series of three talks on the scrolls on the radio in England, in which he contended that Dupont-Sommer "was more right than he knew."[10] Allegro pointed to the pesher on Nahum, which refers to an "angry lion" who "hangs up men alive." This is usually recognized as a reference to the Jewish king Alexander Jannaeus, who crucified hundreds of his enemies in the early first century BCE (Josephus, *Antiquities* 13.380; *Jewish War* 1.97). Allegro identified Jannaeus as the Wicked Priest, the adversary of the teacher. He reasoned that the teacher was one of those crucified. He then continued: "When the Jewish king had left, [the sectarians] took down the broken body of their Master to stand guard over it until Judgment Day. . . . They believed their Master would rise again and lead his faithful flock (the people of the new testament as they called themselves) to a new and purified Jerusalem." This provoked his fellow editors to write a letter to the *Times* of London in which they professed that they were "unable to see in the texts the 'findings' of Mr. Allegro. We find no crucifixion of the 'teacher,' no deposition from the cross, and no 'broken body of their Master' to be stood guard over until Judgment Day. Therefore, there is no 'well-defined Essenic pattern into which Jesus of Nazareth fits,' as Mr. Allegro is alleged in one report to have said."[11]

Thereafter, this phase of the debate subsided. Allegro eventually retired to the Isle of Man and turned his attention to writing *The Sacred Mushroom and the Cross*, in which he argued that the origin of Christianity lay in psychedelic experiences promulgated by an orgiastic mushroom cult.[12]

8. Edmund Wilson, *The Dead Sea Scrolls, 1947–1969* (New York: Oxford University Press, 1969), 98.

9. Ibid., 99.

10. Baigent and Leigh, *Dead Sea Scrolls Deception*, 46.

11. Ibid., 49–50.

12. Ibid., 61. A sympathetic account of Allegro's career by his daughter, Judith Anne Brown, has now been published: *John Marco Allegro: The Maverick of the Dead Sea Scrolls* (Grand Rapids: Eerdmans, 2005).

Renewed Controversy

When the scrolls became generally available in the early 1990s, there were some brief flurries of controversy. Even though the so-called Son of God text (4Q246) had been known to scholars for twenty years, it received fresh headlines in 1992 announcing "a Son of God" before Jesus. A fragment of the War Scroll was initially interpreted as referring to the death of the messiah, but discussion soon showed that the messiah was more likely to be the one doing the killing in that text.[13] Two English authors, Michael Baigent and Richard Leigh, tried to resurrect the charge that the Roman Catholic authors on the editorial team had conspired to suppress discoveries that would damage the credibility of Christianity.[14] But in fact correspondences between the scrolls and the New Testament could just as easily be used to support the Christian faith, by showing that ideas developed in Christianity were indeed current in Judaism around the turn of the era. The kind of debate instigated by Allegro, or revived by Baigent and Leigh, by alleging that the scrolls somehow undermine Christianity, has no substance and is little more than a publicity gimmick.

There remain, however, serious scholarly questions about the development of Christianity out of Judaism. The first Christians were Jews, as was Jesus himself, and we should expect that many of their ideas would find parallels in the Jewish literature of the time. It is also true that there were several messianic pretenders in Judaism in the Roman period. There is no a priori reason why there should not have been a messiah before Jesus. The question is not one of a priori possibility, however, but of historical evidence, and it bears most directly on the interpretation of a few texts from the Dead Sea Scrolls.

Wise and Knohl

The books of Wise and Knohl are both written in popular style, with imaginative recreations of situations in the messiah's life,

13. G. Vermes, "The Oxford Forum for Qumran Research Seminar on the Rule of War from Cave 4 (4Q285)," *Journal of Jewish Studies* 43 (1992): 85–90. See Collins, *Scepter and the Star*, 58–60.

14. Baigent and Leigh, *Dead Sea Scrolls Deception*, 26–66.

but they are serious proposals from scholars with a thorough mastery of the texts. The two books were written quite independently of one another and differ in several important respects. Wise's messiah is the teacher, whom he calls Judah and dates to the reign of Alexander Jannaeus. The crucial events are placed at the end of the teacher's life, in the years 76–73 BCE. Knohl's messiah is not the original teacher, but a later teacher, Menahem the Essene, who is known from Josephus and who was a friend of King Herod (Josephus, *Antiquities* 15.373–79). Wise's messiah is sentenced to death but not executed: his sentence is commuted to exile. Knohl's messiah is killed and his body is thrown in the street. Yet they resemble each other in important ways. Both identify themselves as the Suffering Servant foretold by Isaiah, and both were believed by their followers to have been enthroned in heaven after their death. Knohl's messiah had already spoken of himself as one enthroned in heaven; Wise argues that this claim was imputed to the messiah after his death. In this respect, Knohl's messiah offers a closer parallel to the New Testament.

I do not propose to discuss every aspect of these interesting proposals here. Knohl's book is the more speculative of the two. His identification of the messiah with Menahem the Essene lacks any support in the tradition and requires a further dubious identification with a Menahem who is mentioned in the Mishnah (tractate *Hagigah* 2.2; cf. Jerusalem Talmud, tractate *Hagigah* 2.2 [77b]). Knohl's evidence for the death of the messiah, which he dates to the disturbances in 4 BCE after the death of Herod, is derived from Revelation 11 and from Lactantius's citations and paraphrase of the *Oracle of Hystaspes*. It is far from apparent that either of these texts is a reliable historical source, either for the events after the death of Herod or for any other time. Both accounts are more easily explained as presupposing the death and resurrection of Jesus rather than as Jewish models for the New Testament story.[15] Wise's account of the adventures of the teacher is highly ingenious and is certainly open to debate, but it is based entirely on the interpretation (however speculative) of texts found at Qumran. Here I will focus on the claims that the books have in common: that a figure described in the scrolls

15. See my review of Knohl's book in *Jewish Quarterly Review* 91 (2000): 185–90, reprinted with minor changes as chapter 2 below.

identified himself as the Suffering Servant and was believed to be exalted to heaven and that this figure can appropriately be called a messiah.

The Teacher of Righteousness and the Suffering Servant

The case for the view that a figure at Qumran, specifically the Teacher of Righteousness, identified himself as the Suffering Servant of Isaiah is made in great detail by Wise.[16] The evidence is found in the so-called Teacher Hymns in columns 10–16 of the *Hodayot* (identified as columns 2–8 in the original edition of the *Hodayot*).[17] While the authorship of these hymns is never explicitly indicated, the hypothesis that the speaker is in fact the teacher is plausible, and it will be assumed here for the sake of the argument. It should be noted that the self-designation of the speaker as "servant" is not especially common in these hymns[18] and is more frequent in the remainder of the *Hodayot*, the "Hymns of the Community." The argument for the identification rests on (a) thematic correspondences between the career of the teacher and the portrayal of the servant in Isaiah and (b) allusions to specific passages in the Servant Songs, usually identified as Isaiah 42:1–4; 49:1–7; 50:4–9; and 52:13–53:12 in modern scholarship. In antiquity, however, these passages were not distinguished as a special group of poems,[19] and indeed their distinctiveness has again been questioned in modern times.[20] We

16. For a more detailed critique of Wise's arguments see my "Teacher and Servant," *Revue d'histoire et de philosophie religieuses* 80 (2000): 37–50.

17. Jeremias, *Der Lehrer der Gerechtigkeit*, 168–77; Michael Douglas, "The Teacher Hymn Hypothesis Revisited: New Data for an Old Crux," *Dead Sea Discoveries* 6 (1999): 239–66.

18. Jeremias, *Der Lehrer der Gerechtigkeit*, 305, admits only three such references.

19. J. Jeremias, "Παῖς Θεοῦ," in *Theological Dictionary of the New Testament* (ed. G. Kittel and G. Friedrich; trans. G. W. Bromiley; Grand Rapids: Eerdmans, 1967), 5:682: "First it should be noted that the modern isolation of the Servant Songs, like the division of the book into Proto-, Deutero- and Trito-Isaiah, was completely unknown in that day." The distinction of the Servant Songs originates with Bernhard Duhm, *Das Buch Jesaia* (Göttingen: Vandenhoeck & Ruprecht, 1892).

20. E.g., Richard J. Clifford, *Fair Spoken and Persuading: An Interpretation of Second Isaiah* (New York: Paulist, 1984).

should be wary, then, of assuming that the modern construct of the servant was also recognized in antiquity. The crucial passage for our purpose is Isaiah 52:13–53:12, which describes a figure who is despised and afflicted but who is vindicated by God and makes many righteous by his suffering. But we should also allow for the possibility that an ancient author might combine passages in ways different from the conventions of modern scholarship and that other passages in the book may have been understood to speak about the same figure described in Isaiah 53.

Wise claims that toward the end of the Teacher Hymns, the teacher "came to speak of himself as the Servant of the Lord in concentrated fashion. He made allusion after allusion to the passages of Isaiah that modern scholars designate Servant Songs, and others to portions that might easily be so construed."[21] Some of the allusions he identifies are questionable or relate to passages in Isaiah where the theme of the Suffering Servant is not explicit.[22] But several are clearly valid. 1QH[a] 16 speaks of a shoot (נצר, מטע) nourished by the streams; and Isaiah speaks of the servant as a sapling and a root (יונק, שרש). The terminology is different, but in 16.10–11 we are told that the one who causes this shoot to grow is hidden, without esteem (בלוא נחשב), like the servant in Isaiah 53:3. The shoot in the hymn seems to be the community rather than the teacher, but the teacher is associated with the servant by the lack of esteem.

Again, 1QH[a] 16.26–27 reads: "I sojourn with sickness and my heart is stricken with afflictions. I am like a man forsaken." Isaiah 53:3–4 is translated: "He was despised and forsaken by men, a man of suffering and acquainted with sickness. . . . We accounted him afflicted." There is some common terminology here (חלי ["sickness"], נגע ["stricken"]), although the distinctive phrase of Isaiah, איש מכאבות ("man of sorrows"), is not reproduced. A clearer allusion to Isaiah 53:3, however, is found in 1QH[a] 12.8, where the author complains that "they do not esteem me," using the same verb, חשב, that is used with reference to the servant in the Isaianic passage: "despised, and we did not esteem him." This

---

21. Wise, *First Messiah*, 290.

22. 1QH[a] 15.10: "[You have reinforced me] in your covenant and emboldened my tongue according to your teachings." Wise claims allusions here to Isa. 42:6: "I have given you the covenant of the people, the light of the nations" (cf. 49:8). The last phrase recalls 50:4: "The Lord gave me a disciple's tongue."

allusion is repeated in 1QH^a 12.23. The claim of the hymnist in 12.27, "through me you have enlightened the face of the many [רבים]," may also be taken as an allusion to Isaiah 53:11, which says that the servant will make many (רבים) righteous.

Moreover, there are also some clear allusions to other passages that modern scholars classify as Servant Songs. So, for example, 1QH^a 15.6–7: "I thank you, O Lord, for you have upheld me [סמכתני] by your might and have poured out your holy spirit within me," recalls Isaiah 42:1: "Here is my Servant whom I uphold [אתמך־בו], my chosen, in whom my soul delights; I have put my spirit upon him." The endowment with the spirit also recalls Isaiah 61:1: "The spirit of the LORD God is upon me, because the LORD has anointed me. He has sent me to bring good news to the oppressed." This passage is not conventionally classified with the Servant Songs, but it is also reflected in the *Hodayot*. In 1QH^a 23.14 the speaker says, "You have opened a spring in the mouth of your servant . . . whom you have supported with your power, to [be] according to your truth . . . herald of your goodness, to proclaim to the poor the abundance of your mercies."

While Wise presents a maximalist view of the allusions to the Servant Songs, the parallels are more extensive than are usually allowed. Like the servant, the teacher claims to be endowed with the spirit and to have "a disciple's tongue" (or be a teacher) (1QH^a 15.10; cf. Isa. 50:4), but is rejected and not esteemed, and afflicted with sickness. Nonetheless, his career benefits "the many." Since the same words are used in some of these cases, at the least, it is reasonable to conclude that the teacher drew on Isaiah's depiction of the servant to describe his own situation. It does not necessarily follow that he saw himself as the fulfillment of prophecy. He could be using the words of Isaiah in an allusive way, as is often the case in the *Hodayot*, to suggest an analogy between himself and the servant. But given the way that Scripture is interpreted in the pesharim at Qumran, it is plausible that he did see himself as the servant of whom Isaiah spoke.

The Self-Exaltation Hymn

According to Isaiah 52:13, the servant would be "exalted and lifted up, and shall be very high." The author of the Teacher

Hymns sometimes claims to be already exalted: "I thank you, Lord, because you saved my life from the pit, and from the Sheol of Abaddon have lifted me up to an everlasting height, so that I can walk on a boundless plain" (1QH^a 11.19–20). An even more grandiose claim is found in 4Q427, another hymn that was included in one edition of the *Hodayot*. Other copies of this hymn are found in 4Q491c and 4Q471b, both of which were originally regarded as copies of the *War Scroll*. More precisely, we have two recensions of this hymn, the shorter form in 4Q491c, and the longer in 4Q427 frag. 7 and 4Q471b. Further fragments of the longer recension are found in 4Q431, which is part of the same manuscript as 4Q471b, and in 1QH^a 25.35–26.10.[23]

The recension of the self-glorification hymn found in 4Q491 evidently began with praise of God for his marvelous deeds and went on to speak of "a mighty throne in the congregation of the gods," on which none of the kings of the East shall sit. (The Hebrew term for "gods," אלים, can refer to heavenly beings other than the Most High, so, in effect, to angels.) The speaker boasts: "I am reckoned with the gods, and my dwelling is in the holy congregation," and "there is no teaching comparable [to my teaching]." He boasts that his glory is with the sons of the king (i.e., God). Some other striking phrases are found in the other fragments. The speaker is "beloved of the king, companion of the holy ones" and even asks "who is like me among the gods?" (4Q471b).

Most of the discussion of this hymn focuses on the identity of the speaker in the self-glorification part. There is no parallel for such self-glorification on the part of a human being in ancient Judaism—the closest parallel is perhaps the self-praise of Wisdom in Sirach 24. Accordingly, the first editor, Maurice Baillet, felt that the speaker must be an angel and dubbed the

---

23. For a comprehensive discussion see E. Eshel, "The Identification of the 'Speaker' of the Self-Glorification Hymn," in *The Provo International Conference on the Dead Sea Scrolls* (ed. D. W. Parry and E. Ulrich; Leiden: Brill, 1999); M. O. Wise, "מי כמוני באלים: A Study of 4Q491c, 4Q471b, 4Q427 7, and 1QH^a 25:35–26:10," *Dead Sea Discoveries* 7 (2000): 173–219. See also J. J. Collins and D. Dimant, "A Thrice-Told Hymn: A Response to Eileen Schuller," *Jewish Quarterly Review* 85 (1994): 151–55; and D. Dimant, "A Synoptic Comparison of Parallel Sections in 4Q427 7, 4Q491 11, and 4Q471b," *Jewish Quarterly Review* 85 (1994): 157–61.

piece "the canticle of Michael."[24] As the late Morton Smith rather caustically observed, however, an archangel would not need to boast about being reckoned with the "gods" or heavenly beings. The speaker must be a human being.[25] Those who seek a human author usually suggest the Teacher of Righteousness, who is the only personality about whom we know anything in the Dead Sea sect.[26] In this case the suggestion is supported by the hymn's boast about the author's teaching. But the tone of this hymn is very different from that of the so-called Teacher Hymns. There is no reflection here on being a creature of clay; on the contrary, the author boasts that his desire is not like that of flesh. Consequently two other suggestions are made. The author might not be *the* teacher, but a later teacher in the history of the sect.[27] Knohl identifies him with his messiah, Menahem the Essene.[28] Alternatively, the speaker may not be a historical person at all but an ideal, imaginary one, such as the eschatological high priest who would also hold a teaching office.[29] He is not explicitly identified as a messiah, although being enthroned in heaven is quite compatible with either the kingly messiah (cf. Ps. 110) or the priestly one.[30] None of these suggestions, however, commands a consensus. Identification with

24. M. Baillet, *Qumrân grotte 4.III* (Discoveries in the Judaean Desert 7; Oxford: Clarendon, 1982), 26–29.

25. M. Smith, "Ascent to the Heavens and Deification in 4QMª," in *Archaeology and History in the Dead Sea Scrolls* (ed. L. H. Schiffman; Sheffield: JSOT Press, 1990), 181–88.

26. E.g., M. G. Abegg Jr., "Who Ascended to Heaven? 4Q491, 4Q427, and the Teacher of Righteousness," in *Eschatology, Messianism, and the Dead Sea Scrolls* (ed. C. A. Evans and P. W. Flint; Grand Rapids: Eerdmans, 1997), 61–73; cf. Wise, "מי כמוני באלים," 218.

27. I explore this possibility in "A Throne in the Heavens: Apotheosis in Pre-Christian Judaism," in *Death, Ecstasy, and Otherworldly Journeys* (ed. J. J. Collins and M. Fishbane; Albany: SUNY Press, 1995), 43–58.

28. Knohl, *Messiah before Jesus*, 52–68.

29. Collins, *Scepter and the Star*, 148; Eshel, "Identification of the 'Speaker.'" See, however, the objection of Crispin H. T. Fletcher-Lewis (*All the Glory of Adam: Liturgical Anthropology in the Dead Sea Scrolls* [Leiden: Brill, 2002], 199–216), who argues that the hymn reflects the liturgical life of the community and is not eschatological.

30. The figure enthroned in Ps. 110 is also a priest forever according to the order of Melchizedek. In the Epistle to the Hebrews, Jesus is associated with a throne of grace and with Ps. 110 precisely as high priest.

the (or a) teacher is not impossible and is perhaps as plausible as any other interpretation.

A more fundamental question, for our present purpose, concerns the relation of the figure in the scroll fragment to the Suffering Servant of Isaiah. Esti Eshel reads 4Q491 frag. 11 1.8–9 as follows:

> Who has been accounted despicable like me? Yet who is like me in my glory? . . . Who has born[e all] afflictions like me, who compares to me [in enduri]ng evil?[31]

In 4Q471b 2–3 she reads:

> Wh[o has been accounted despicable like me? And who] has been oppressed like [me? And who] has been shunned [by men] like [me?

She reconstructs 4Q427 frag. 1 lines 6–7 as follows:

> [Who has been accounted despicable like me? And who has been oppressed like me? And who has been shunned by men like me? And who compare]s to me [in enduring] evil?[32]

Knohl offers a synthetic reconstruction:

> [Who] has been despised like [me? And who] has been rejected [of men] like me? [And who] compares to m[e in enduring] evil?[33]

It should be noted, however, that the passage from 4Q427 is almost entirely reconstructed on the basis of the parallel texts. Eileen Schuller's version reads:

> is despised like me
> like me; and there ceases evil.[34]

---

31. Eshel, "Identification of the 'Speaker,'" 622. She restores 4Q427 frag. 1 lines 6–7 on the basis of this passage.

32. Ibid., 624.

33. Knohl, *Messiah before Jesus*, 15, 23–24.

34. E. G. Chazon et al., eds., *Qumran Cave 4.XX: Poetical and Liturgical Texts, Part 2* (Discoveries in the Judaean Desert 29; Oxford: Clarendon, 1999), 99. These lines are paralleled in 4Q431 frag. 1.

The strongest case for allusions to the Servant Songs is in 4Q491 frag. 11 1.8–9, where we find the phrase ‫[מ]י‬‫א‬ ‫לבוז נחשב‬ ‫בי‬‫א‬ ("who is deemed despicable like me [*or* because of me]?"). Isaiah 53:3 reads: ‫נבזה ולא חשבנהו‬ ("he was despised and we did not esteem him"). The Hebrew phrases have two words in common, ‫חשב‬ ("to deem, esteem") and ‫נבזה/בוז‬ ("to despise"). The references to bearing evils in the following line in 4Q491 are based on the obscure word ‫צערים‬ and the word ‫רע‬ ("evil"), which could also be pointed differently as *rēaʿ* ("friend"). The verbs have to be restored. The phrase translated by Eshel as "shunned by men," ‫חדל אישים‬, is found in Isaiah 53:3. The word ‫חדל‬ is attested in 4Q471b and in 4Q431 frag. 1, but is translated "cease" ("evil will cease") by Schuller, in accordance with the normal meaning of the verb. Both the Servant Song and the Qumran hymn also use the language of exaltation. While there is some uncertainty because of the fragmentary nature of the hymn, it seems safe to say that the author wished to evoke an analogy between himself and the servant, insofar as both were despised but are now exalted. There is no suggestion, however, that the figure in the exaltation hymn atones for sin.

The pattern of being despised and then exalted is similar to what we find elsewhere in the *Hodayot*, but it is, as Knohl rightly insists, exceptional in the degree of exaltation that is claimed. Knohl claims that the figure in the exaltation hymn thought of himself as the Son of Man who sits in heaven on a mighty throne. The figure of the Son of Man seated on a throne of glory is found in the *Similitudes of Enoch*, a text from around the turn of the era that is not attested at Qumran.[35] The Son of Man takes on some attributes of the servant described in Isaiah. He is called the Elect or Chosen One, and he is hidden since the creation of the world (*1 Enoch* 62.7). He is also a light to the nations (48.4). His manifestation in glory will astonish his enemies (62.3–5). He is not, however, a suffering figure, and he is a preexistent heavenly figure, not an exalted human being.[36] He vindicates those who are without esteem in this world, but he is not him-

35. See Collins, *Scepter and the Star*, 177–82.

36. This point is admittedly disputed, as some scholars identify him with the exalted Enoch. See, e.g., J. C. VanderKam, "Righteous One, Messiah, Chosen One, and Son of Man," in *The Messiah* (ed. J. H. Charlesworth; Minneapolis: Fortress, 1992), 169–91. Enoch appears to be identified with the Son of Man in *1 Enoch*

self subjected to contempt or death. It seems, then, that a link between the figure in the exaltation hymn and the *Similitudes of Enoch* is improbable. It seems quite gratuitous to introduce the title Son of Man into the Qumran fragment.

In summary, the figure in the exaltation hymn, who may or may not be the Teacher of Righteousness, is associated with the Suffering Servant, insofar as he suffers contempt but is gloriously exalted. The same could be said of Jesus. It is not apparent, however, that the sufferings of the figure in the hymn from Qumran are regarded as vicarious, in the manner of the servant or in the manner of Jesus.

Servant and Messiah

But was the servant regarded as a messianic figure in pre-Christian Judaism? Despite the stubborn philological arguments of Joseph Fitzmyer,[37] reference to a messianic figure does not necessarily require the word מָשִׁיחַ ("messiah," or "anointed") in every instance, but the use of the word מָשִׁיחַ can serve as a guide to the range of messianic expectation. The word is used in the Dead Sea Scrolls with reference to three distinct kinds of people:[38] (1) the royal messiah, the מְשִׁיחַ יִשְׂרָאֵל ("messiah of Israel"), also called "the branch of David" or "the prince of the congregation," who was expected to drive out the Gentiles and restore the kingdom of Israel; (2) the priestly messiah, the מְשִׁיחַ אַהֲרֹן ("messiah/anointed of Aaron"), who was expected to restore and preside over the legitimate temple worship; and (3) prophets (CD 2.12; 6.1; 1QM 11.7).[39] I argue elsewhere that the messiah whom heaven and earth obey in

---

71.14, in an epilogue, but the identification does not seem to be presupposed in the body of the work.

37. J. A. Fitzmyer, *The Dead Sea Scrolls and Christian Origins* (Grand Rapids: Eerdmans, 2000), 73–110.

38. See Collins, *Scepter and the Star*; J. Zimmermann, *Messianische Texte aus Qumran* (Wissenschaftliche Untersuchungen zum Neuen Testament 2.104; Tübingen: Mohr-Siebeck, 1998); G. G. Xeravits, *King, Priest, Prophet: Positive Eschatological Protagonists of the Qumran Library* (Studies on the Texts of the Desert of Judah 47; Leiden: Brill, 2002).

39. *Pace* J. C. Poirier, "The Endtime Return of Elijah and Moses at Qumran," *Dead Sea Discoveries* 10 (2003): 230–31, the prophetic reference is clear from the context in each case.

4Q521 is a prophetic figure, modeled on Elijah.[40] 11QMelchizedek 2.18 refers to someone "anointed by the spirit," who is identified with the "herald of good news" mentioned in Isaiah 61:1.[41] When we speak of a messianic figure in modern usage, however, it is not enough that a figure be referred to as a מָשִׁיחַ. It is also implied that the figure in question plays a decisive role in the events of the end time. In the case of a prophetic messiah, this is the role of the herald who announces and prepares the way for the new order that is to be ushered in by the messiahs of Aaron and Israel.

The identity of the servant in Second Isaiah, in its original context, is a matter of perennial dispute. Most scholars think that the servant is Israel, but some argue that he is the prophet, and some that he is the king.[42] (Kings in the ancient Near East were often described as "servants" of a god.) The meaning of these passages in their original context, however, is not what concerns us here. Many passages in the Hebrew Bible took on messianic significance in the Second Temple period. Isaiah's prophecy of the root from the stump of Jesse (Isa. 11) was arguably messianic from the start. Balaam's oracle about the scepter and star, in Numbers 24:17, was not, but it too was widely understood as a prediction of either one or two messiahs. In early Christianity, Isaiah 53 took on messianic significance, because it was regarded as a prophecy of the passion and death of Jesus. It is not apparent, however, that Isaiah 53 was understood as a messianic prediction before the crucifixion of Jesus.

Three texts might be adduced as evidence in favor of a messianic understanding of the servant in pre-Christian Judaism. One is the Great Isaiah Scroll from Qumran (1QIsaᵃ).[43] In Isaiah 52:14, where the Masoretic Text reads כֵּן־מִשְׁחַת מֵאִישׁ מַרְאֵהוּ

---

40. Collins, *Scepter and the Star*, 117–23; idem, "The Works of the Messiah," *Dead Sea Discoveries* 1 (1994): 98–112. The attempt of Poirier, "Endtime Return," 221–42, to cast Elijah in the role of end-time priest rather than prophet relies heavily on much later rabbinic traditions.

41. See further J. J. Collins, "A Herald of Good Tidings: Isaiah 61:1–3 and Its Actualization in the Dead Sea Scrolls," in *The Quest for Context and Meaning: Studies in Biblical Intertextuality in Honor of James A. Sanders* (ed. C. A. Evans and S. Talmon; Leiden: Brill, 1997), 225–40.

42. See J. Blenkinsopp, *A History of Prophecy in Israel* (rev. ed.; Louisville: Westminster John Knox, 1996), 189–93.

43. D. Barthélemy, "Le grand rouleau d'Isaïe trouvé près de la Mer Morte," *Revue biblique* 57 (1950): 530–49, esp. 546–49.

("so his appearance was destroyed beyond that of a man"), the Isaiah Scroll reads כ] משחתי ("so I have anointed [his appearance beyond that of a man]"). It is possible that this reading, which dates to the third century BCE, originated either as a scribal error or as a conflated reading,[44] but it lent itself inevitably to a messianic reading, especially if it was read in conjunction with Isaiah 61, where the prophet says that God has anointed him. Whether the teacher read the text this way is an open question. Wise argues that the author of the Teacher Hymns depends on this Isaiah Scroll at several points.[45] But he readily admits that the hymnist did not always follow this text of Isaiah and does not allude to this specific passage. At no point does the author of the *Hodayot* claim to have been anointed, in any sense.

A second text adduced in this regard is the targum of Isaiah, which is no earlier than the second century CE, but may contain old exegetical traditions.[46] At Isaiah 42:1, some manuscripts gloss the word עבדי ("my servant") as משיחא ("the messiah").[47] The reading עבדי משיחא is well attested for Isaiah 52:13. The targum of Isaiah 53, however, consistently changes the meaning of the biblical text, so that the servant is not suffering, but triumphant. His enemies suffer. The temple is destroyed "for our sins." The servant will lead the wicked to slaughter and deliver them to Gehenna.[48] The targum, then, identifies the servant as

44. Brownlee, "Servant of the Lord," 10–11, suggests a conflation of משחת ("marred") and שחתי ("I marred").

45. Wise, *First Messiah*, 94: "Reading the Great Isaiah Scroll, we are face-to-face with a book once consulted—or more likely owned—by . . . the Teacher of Righteousness." He lists readings common to the *Hodayot* and 1QIsa[a] on pp. 291–92.

46. J. Ådna, "The Servant of Isaiah 53 as Triumphant and Interceding Messiah: The Reception of Isaiah 52:13–53:12 in the Targum of Isaiah with Special Attention to the Concept of the Messiah," in *The Suffering Servant: Isaiah 53 in Jewish and Christian Sources* (ed. B. Janowski and P. Stuhlmacher; Grand Rapids: Eerdmans, 2004), 189–224, esp. 194–97, argues for an extended period of composition, but dates the targum of Isa. 53 to the period before Bar Kokhba, because of the messianic expectation. This criterion, however, is very questionable.

47. A. Sperber, *The Bible in Aramaic*, vol. 3: *The Latter Prophets according to Targum Jonathan* (Leiden: Brill, 1962), 84; and C. A. Evans, *Jesus and His Contemporaries* (Leiden: Brill, 1995), 165.

48. Jeremias, "Παῖς Θεοῦ," 693–95; B. D. Chilton, *The Isaiah Targum* (Aramaic Bible 11; Wilmington, DE: Glazier, 1987), 103–5; and Evans, *Jesus and His Contemporaries*, 166.

messiah, but ignores the theme of suffering or refers it to other figures. It provides a salutary reminder that ancient exegetes did not necessarily read texts in the ways that seem obvious to their modern counterparts.

Finally, the Son of Man in the *Similitudes of Enoch* is also called "my messiah" or "my anointed one" (*1 Enoch* 48.10; 52.4). As we have seen, the *Similitudes* borrows language associated with Isaiah's servant to describe the messianic Son of Man, but it does not attribute to him the suffering of the servant.

The Servant Song of Isaiah 52–53 is invoked in pre-Christian Judaism primarily as a paradigm of humiliation and exaltation. In Daniel 11–12, the teachers who are martyred in the time of persecution are called משכילים, an allusion to Isaiah 52:13: הנה ישכיל עבדי ("behold, my servant will prosper"). These people instruct "the many." Some of them are killed in the course of the persecution, but they are subsequently raised and shine like the stars, just as the servant is said to be "very high" in Isaiah 52:13. Similarly, in the Wisdom of Solomon the righteous one is called *pais theou*, which can mean either servant or child of God. This figure is humiliated and put to death, but is gloriously vindicated at the judgment to the astonishment of his enemies. There is no suggestion, however, that the righteous suffer vicariously, either in Daniel or in the Wisdom of Solomon, and there is no suggestion that they are messiahs, in any sense of the word.

In summary, allusions to the Servant Songs do not in themselves establish messianic claims on the part of the Teacher of Righteousness. The argument for such claims would be strengthened if it could be shown that the teacher identified himself with the speaker in Isaiah 61:1–3 ("the spirit of the Lord God is upon me, because the Lord has anointed me; he has sent me to bring good news to the oppressed"). As we have seen earlier, this passage is evoked in 1QHᵃ 23.14: "You have opened a spring in the mouth of your servant . . . whom you have supported with your power, to [be] according to your truth . . . herald of your goodness, to proclaim to the poor the abundance of your mercies." This passage is not found in the supposed Teacher Hymns, but it may suggest that some followers of the teacher, at least, saw this passage as part of the profile of the servant/prophet.

The Eschatological Prophet?

Isaiah 61 is taken to refer to eschatological events in 11QMelchizedek and 4Q521.[49] 11QMelchizedek 2.18 speaks of a herald who is "the anointed of the spirit," who announces salvation and comforts the afflicted. Some scholars think that this herald is Melchizedek himself,[50] but he is more easily identified as a prophetic precursor of Melchizedek.[51] In 4Q521, preaching good news to the poor is included in the works of the Lord, but it is most probably the work of a prophetic agent. The text refers to a messiah or anointed one whom heaven and earth obey. Since the herald who preaches good news is an anointed prophet in Isaiah 61, it is reasonable to infer that the anointed one has the same function in 4Q521.[52] In both cases, the anointed prophet of Isaiah 61 is understood as an eschatological messianic figure. There is ample evidence that the Teacher of Righteousness, or the author of the Teacher Hymns, saw himself as a prophet.[53] Should we conclude that he saw himself as an eschatological messianic prophet?

Quite apart from the connection with the Servant Songs, several scholars suggest that the teacher was understood as the eschatological prophet.[54] As Vermes argues: "If . . . the messianic Prophet (or prophetic Messiah) was to teach the truth revealed on the eve of the establishment of the Kingdom, it would follow that his part was to all intents and purposes to be the same as that attributed by the Essenes to the Teacher of Righteousness."[55] The teacher was evidently a prophet who heralded the coming of the end of days, and there is some

49. Collins, "Herald of Good Tidings."
50. So Wise, *First Messiah*, 231.
51. Florentino García Martínez, "Messianische Erwartungen in den Qumranschriften," *Jahrbuch für biblische Theologie* 8 (1993): 203; and M. de Jonge and A. S. van der Woude, "11QMelchizedek and the New Testament," *New Testament Studies* 12 (1965–66): 307.
52. Collins, *Scepter and the Star*, 117–22.
53. Dupont-Sommer, *Essene Writings from Qumran*, 360–64.
54. N. Wieder, "The 'Law Interpreter' of the Sect of the Dead Sea Scrolls: The Second Moses," *Journal of Jewish Studies* 4 (1953): 158–75; and G. Vermes, *The Dead Sea Scrolls: Qumran in Perspective* (Philadelphia: Fortress, 1981), 185–86.
55. Vermes, *Dead Sea Scrolls*, 185–86.

evidence that his followers believed that the final period of history had already begun.[56]

Nonetheless there are problems with the view that the teacher was believed to be the eschatological prophet. The form of the *Community Rule* found in 1QS is usually assumed to presuppose the activity of the teacher, although it does not refer to him. Yet it famously refers to "the coming of the prophet and the messiahs of Aaron and Israel" as a future event (1QS 9.11). The *Damascus Document*, which explicitly refers to the death of the teacher, distinguishes between an interpreter of the law, who appears to be already in the past, and one who "teaches righteousness at the end of days," who is still in the future (CD 6.7–11).[57] In other texts, however, the interpreter of the law is a future eschatological figure (4Q174 1.11). "Teacher" and "interpreter" were functions, fulfilled at one time by the historical teacher and at a future time by an eschatological prophet. The two figures are similar, but nonetheless distinguished. So, while the teacher may well have considered himself to be an anointed prophet or servant, it is misleading to speak of him as the eschatological prophet or as a messiah, in the definitive eschatological sense. It remains significant that he does not refer to himself as anointed in the *Hodayot*.

Conclusion

Much of the controversy initiated by Dupont-Sommer over fifty years ago—and revived by the theses of Wise and Knohl—is concerned with the degree of resemblance between the Essene teacher and Jesus. Jesus too was a prophet, sometimes mistaken for Elijah redivivus (e.g., Mark 8:28). According to Luke, he claimed to be the figure prophesied in Isaiah 61, who preached good news to the poor and performed works of mercy (Luke 4:18–19). His death and exaltation were seen as the fulfillment of the Suffering Servant prophecies in Isaiah.

Nonetheless, there were several crucial differences. In the case of Jesus, identification as the servant meant that his suf-

---

56. A. Steudel, "אחרית הימים in the Texts from Qumran," *Revue de Qumran* 62 (1993): 225–46.

57. See Collins, *Scepter and the Star*, 112–14.

fering and death were regarded as vicarious atonement for the sins of others. This was not the case with the teacher. In 1QH[a] 10.8–9, the speaker claims to be a trap for sinners but a healing (מרפא) for all who turn away from sin. There is no suggestion, however, that the healing is brought about by the suffering of the teacher. In fact, we have no evidence that Isaiah 53 was understood in terms of vicarious suffering in pre-Christian Judaism. The teacher, like the *maśkîlîm* in Daniel, suffers in the course of fulfilling his mission to others, but there is no indication that his suffering functions as atonement.[58]

A second crucial difference concerns the expectation of the role that Jesus and the teacher would play in the eschatological future. Not only did Jesus's followers believe that he was taken up and enthroned in heaven after his death, they also believed that he would come again on the clouds of heaven as the Son of Man, to destroy the wicked and preside over the final judgment. In the scrolls, a similar eschatological role is filled by Melchizedek, who is said to execute the judgments of God. Despite the attempt of Wise to identify Melchizedek as "the anointed of the spirit," who might then be identified with the teacher as eschatological prophet, it seems clear that these figures are distinct in the scroll from Qumran. There is no suggestion in the scrolls that the teacher would come again. In fact, the figure of the Son of Man, described in Daniel 7, is surprisingly absent from the scrolls, despite the prominence there of the book of Daniel. It is possible, but not certain, that the figure who is called the Son of God in 4Q246 is based on an interpretation of the one like a Son of Man in Daniel 7. But that figure is a kingly messiah, who conforms to the standard expectation of a divinely aided warrior who will bring about a lasting era of peace.[59]

58. The idea of atonement appears in 4Q541, a fragmentary Aramaic text that uses motifs associated with the Suffering Servant to describe a future figure who will atone for the sin of his generation. This figure should be identified as the eschatological high priest, and presumably he will make atonement by the appropriate rituals, not by his own suffering. See Collins, *Scepter and the Star*, 123–26.

59. Ibid., 154–72. The association with Dan. 7 is disputed by J. D. G. Dunn, "'Son of God' as 'Son of Man' in the Dead Sea Scrolls? A Response to John Collins on 4Q246," in *The Scrolls and the Scriptures: Qumran Fifty Years After* (ed. S. E. Porter and C. A. Evans; Journal for the Study of the Pseudepigrapha Supplement 26; Sheffield: Sheffield Academic Press, 1997), 198–209.

There was, of course, another fundamental difference between Jesus of Nazareth and the teachers of the Essene sect. This lay in the nature of their teachings. The sectarian teaching focused on purity and the exact fulfillment of the Torah. The teaching of Jesus, as preserved in the Gospels, focused on the spirit of the law and relativized ideas of purity. Essenism and early Christianity were both products of the same culture and society and shared many beliefs about messianic expectation and the end of days.[60] The famous dictum of Renan, cited approvingly by Dupont-Sommer, held that Christianity was "an Essenism that has largely succeeded."[61] But this dictum was wide of the mark. It would have been truer to say that Christianity was an anti-Essenism that succeeded because it rejected the inward turn of the older sect, with its obsession with purity, and sought instead to spread its message to the broader world.[62]

60. See further J. J. Collins, "Qumran, Apocalypticism, and the New Testament," in *The Dead Sea Scrolls Fifty Years after Their Discovery* (ed. L. H. Schiffman, E. Tov, and J. C. VanderKam; Jerusalem: Israel Exploration Society, 2000), 133–38.

61. Dupont-Sommer, *Essene Writings from Qumran*, 370.

62. Compare my remarks in "Qumran, Apocalypticism, and the New Testament."

2

AN ESSENE MESSIAH?

COMMENTS ON ISRAEL KNOHL,
THE MESSIAH BEFORE JESUS

John J. Collins

Israel Knohl's book *The Messiah before Jesus* cannot be faulted for lack of originality or for any timidity about putting forth bold hypotheses. According to Knohl, a Jewish messiah of the Essene sect lived and died a generation or so before Jesus and anticipated his career in some uncanny ways. This figure conceived himself after the model of the Suffering Servant and claimed to be vindicated and exalted to heaven. During the revolt after the death of Herod, however, he and another lesser figure were put to death, and their bodies left in the street for three days. After this he was believed to have been taken up to heaven. The death of Jesus was later understood according to this paradigm. Amazingly, no record of this Essene messiah survived, and he remained unknown to history for two thousand years.

An earlier version of this essay appeared in *Jewish Quarterly Review* 91 (2000): 185–90 and is reprinted here by permission.

Knohl's argument depends on several identifications that are essentially intuitive—he does not engage in much critical discussion of his primary texts or consider alternative interpretations or counter possible objections. If we are to do justice to his thesis, however, we need to engage in precisely this kind of critical discussion. I will focus briefly on four texts: the self-glorification hymn in 4Q491, the *Oracle of Hystaspes*, Revelation 11, and 4Q246, the Son of God text.

The self-glorification hymn is an exceedingly difficult text, and I have vacillated over its interpretation. The speaker is not explicitly identified as a messiah. Messianic identity may be implied, as I among others suggest, but it is not certain. If he is a messiah, he seems more likely to be a priestly messiah than a royal one, in view of the emphasis on his teaching. Knohl opts for a kingly character, because of his throne in heaven (cf. Ps. 110), but the figure enthroned in Psalm 110 is also a priest forever according to the order of Melchizedek. In the Epistle to the Hebrews, Jesus is associated with a throne of grace and with Psalm 110 precisely as high priest. Apart from the throne, there is nothing in the self-glorification hymn that suggests a kingly messiah. A more fundamental question, however, concerns the relation of the figure in the scroll fragment to the Suffering Servant of Isaiah. There is no doubt that the scroll alludes to Isaiah 53 when it asks, "Who has been despised like me?" But does this amount to an identification with the Suffering Servant, so that we can infer that this figure atones for sin? Such an inference is risky at best. It is true that the Qumran pesharim use a method of interpretation that involves identifying figures mentioned in Scripture with historical persons. But we also find in the scrolls a more allusive use of Scripture, and all scriptural interpretation at Qumran is atomistic. An allusion to Isaiah 53 in the matter of being despised does not necessarily entail a claim that the contempt suffered atones for sin. The figure in the self-glorification hymn claims to have been despised but to be now exalted. This claim is similar to a pattern that we otherwise find in the *Hodayot*, but it is, as Knohl rightly insists, exceptional in the degree of exaltation that is claimed. Knohl's claim that this figure thought of himself as the Son of Man who sits in heaven on a mighty throne requires an allusion to the *Similitudes of Enoch*, which seems improbable. It seems quite gratuitous to introduce the title Son of Man into the Qumran fragment. In summary, 4Q491 may be messianic, although this is not certain. There is some similarity to Jesus in the pattern of contempt followed by exaltation, but this similarity does not extend to an atoning function or to an identification with the (Danielic) Son of Man. It seems misleading to say that the figure is identified with the Suffering Servant.

In his attempt to create a context for understanding the Qumran fragment, Knohl introduces the *Oracle of Hystaspes*. In this he is to be commended; the oracle is certainly relevant to discussions of Jewish messianism and is seldom brought into the discussion. It is unfortunate, however, that Knohl seems to accept uncritically the idiosyncratic view of David Flusser that the oracle is Jewish. This text—quoted by early-fourth-century Christian church father Lactantius—is ostensibly and plausibly of Persian origin. There is no compelling reason to posit a Jewish stage in its transmission. The reconstruction of the actual text of Hystaspes, however, is problematic. Lactantius cites Hystaspes explicitly some eight times. Scholars suspect more extensive use of the oracle, but differ as to how much of Lactantius's text should be ascribed to Hystaspes. Knohl seems to follow the rather maximalist view of Flusser. I prefer the more cautious assessment of John Hinnells.[1] The prophecy about the two kings, one of whom would rule over Asia and the other of whom would be worshiped as Son of God, is not attributed to Hystaspes by Lactantius (*Divine Institutes* 7.16.4; 7.17.4). Knohl boldly identifies the king who will rule over Asia as Mark Antony, but this is problematic if we read the whole passage:

> Then civil discords will perpetually be sown; nor will there be any rest from deadly wars, until ten kings arise at the same time, who will divide the world, not to govern, but to consume it. . . . Then a most powerful enemy will suddenly arise against him from the extreme boundaries of the northern region, who, having destroyed three of that number who shall then be in possession of Asia, shall be admitted into alliance by the others, and shall be constituted

1. John R. Hinnells, "The Zoroastrian Doctrine of Salvation in the Roman World: A Study of the Oracle of Hystaspes," in *Man and His Salvation: Studies in Memory of S. G. F. Brandon* (ed. E. J. Sharpe and J. R. Hinnells; Manchester: Manchester University Press, 1973), 125–48.

prince of all. He shall harass the world with an intolerable rule; shall mingle things divine and human; . . . he will change the laws and appoint his own; he will contaminate, plunder, spoil, and put to death. And at length, the name being changed and the seat of government being transferred, confusion and the disturbance of mankind will follow.[2]

If this is prophecy after the fact, then the seat of government must already have been transferred. It is not clear who the ten kings could be in the context of Mark Antony's lifetime or why an enemy should be said to come from the extreme boundaries of the north. It seems much more plausible that this passage is a genuinely eschatological oracle of a type that we often find in the *Sibylline Oracles*, which weaves together several traditional motifs. A "king from Asia" is a well-known motif in these oracles (also in the *Potter's Oracle*) as are the ten kings (to which we may also compare the ten horns of the fourth beast in Dan. 7).

In the case of the second king in Lactantius, it is also important to read the whole passage (*Divine Institutes* 7.17.4):

When the close of the times draws nigh, a great prophet shall be sent from God to turn men to the knowledge of God and he shall receive the power of doing wonderful things. Wherever men shall not hear him, he will shut up the heaven, and cause it to withhold its rains; he will turn their water into blood and torment them with thirst and hunger . . . and when his works shall be accomplished, another king shall arise out of Syria, born from an evil spirit, the overthrower and destroyer of the human race, who shall destroy that which is left by the former evil, together with himself. He shall fight against the prophet of God, and shall overcome and slay him, and shall suffer him to lie unburied; but after the third day he shall come to life again, and while all look on and wonder, he shall be caught up into heaven. But that king will not only be most disgraceful in himself, but he will also be a prophet of lies; and he will constitute and call himself God, and will order himself to be worshiped as the Son of God; and power will be given him to do signs and wonders, by the sight of which he may entice men to adore him. He will command fire to come

---

2. Lactantius, *The Divine Institutes* 7.16, in *The Ante-Nicene Fathers: Translations of the Writings of the Fathers down to A.D. 325* (ed. Alexander Roberts and James Donaldson; Grand Rapids: Eerdmans, 1985), 7:213.

down from heaven, and the sun to stand and leave his course, and an image to speak; and these things shall be done at his word and by these things even the wise will be enticed by him. Then he will attempt to destroy the temple of God and persecute the righteous people; and there will be distress and tribulation such as there never has been from the beginning of the world.[3]

Knohl argues that the false prophet is Augustus, but then, why is he said to arise out of Syria? And what is the basis for the claim that Augustus did miracles? Any interpretation of this text must begin with its meaning in the context of Lactantius. Here the false prophet is clearly an antichrist figure: he is called Son of God because Christ was called Son of God; and he is also the mirror image of Christ in other respects. In my view, this is not prophecy after the fact, but an eschatological prophecy in the anthological style found in many writers of the patristic period, such as Pseudo-Methodius or Pseudo-Ephraem, who try to weave together various eschatological traditions into a synthetic narrative. It is part of a rich antichrist tradition in patristic and medieval literature. It is certainly possible that some of these traditions originally had historical referents, but the recovery of these references is difficult. In this case, the depiction of the antichrist figure or false prophet seems clearly to presuppose early Christian texts, especially the book of Revelation. The only motif here that might seem to require a pre-Christian date is the reference to the destruction of the temple of God. But the destruction or desecration of the temple was an important motif in biblical texts of both Testaments (Daniel, 2 Thessalonians) and remained prominent in Christian eschatological prophecy down to the Middle Ages. Most often, it was understood as "the temple of the church" (so, e.g., Joachim of Fiore). Such motifs have their origin in historical events, but they are reinterpreted and projected into the future. An allusion to such a motif is not necessarily to be taken as a fragment of a historical source. The main point I want to make here is that more critical study of Lactantius is necessary before his text can be mined for supposed sources.

3. Ibid., 214.

Knohl notes that a parallel tradition is found in Revelation 11. This should hardly surprise us. Revelation was a major source for Lactantius, even though he departs from it here in speaking of a single prophet instead of two prophetic witnesses. Knohl reads Revelation 11 as a reflection of events in the time of Varus. Revelation 11 begins with a command to measure the temple of God, but not the outer court, "for it is given over to the nations, and they will trample over the holy city for forty-two months." Knohl claims that this corresponds exactly to what happened in 4 BCE, when Roman soldiers set fire to the porticos of the temple, but did not destroy the inner precincts. But he conveniently omits the last phrase of the verse, "for forty-two months," which does not correspond to that incident. The reference to the forty-two months (three and a half years; or a time, times, and half a time) shows that we are dealing here with prophecy. There may be a reminiscence here of a historical attack on the temple (Wellhausen thought it was an oracle from the siege of Jerusalem in the First Revolt) but it is taken up and reused, and it does not follow that every other motif in the passage derives from the same context.

The two witnesses are identified with the two olive trees of Zechariah. Since Zechariah was referring to a royal and a priestly figure, Knohl concludes that they must be a royal and a priestly messiah here too. But he fails to allow for the possibility that a prophecy may be reinterpreted. In fact both figures are prophets; neither figure is a king or a priest (unless we take the motif of fire coming from their mouths as royal by association with Isa. 11). The obvious prototypes are Elijah, who shut up the sky, and Moses, who turned water into blood and brought on the plagues. The eschatological return of Elijah is a well-known motif. Moses had also disappeared at the end of his life and so might also be available for an eschatological cameo. Since the biblical models are so clear, there is no need to invent a historical prototype. That they are killed and then resurrected after three days and taken up to heaven is surely modeled on the fate of Jesus, even though they differ insofar as they are not buried. Their ascent is followed by a great earthquake in which a tenth of the city fell. No such catastrophe is recorded in connection with the campaign of Varus.

It seems, then, quite gratuitous to suppose that the story of the two witnesses records a historical event that is otherwise unknown. Josephus gives a full account of the campaign of Varus, and he has a keen interest in messianic pretenders, even in a relatively obscure figure such as Athronges. Why would he fail to mention the supposed Essene messiah? It is also gratuitous to assume that these traditions came from the Qumran sect or some circle close to them. Where do we find such a tradition in the Dead Sea Scrolls? Neither 4Q491 nor any other Qumran text says anything about the killing of a messiah (despite the controversy over the pierced messiah text) or about his resurrection after three days. The only connection that I can see between Revelation 11 and the scrolls is that both have the motif of two messiahs, but in Revelation these are two prophets while in the scrolls they are messiahs of Aaron and Israel.

The argument that the speaker in the self-glorification hymn should be identified with Menahem the Essene is independent of this reconstruction of events in the time of Varus. Since we are never told that this Menahem was put to death as a messianic pretender, the identification would be less problematic apart from that reconstruction. It is still problematic, and Knohl is rightly tentative about it. Is it reasonable to suppose that the Menahem paired with Hillel was an Essene? Is this compatible with what we know (or think we know) about relations between the Essenes and the Pharisees? The attempt to find a real-life author for the self-glorification hymn is intriguing, and Knohl's suggestion cannot be disproved, but neither can it be established with any degree of probability. It is an interesting suggestion, to be left on the table pending further evidence to confirm or refute it.

Finally, a word about 4Q246. The suggestions that the Son of God figure is a Syrian king are not remotely plausible. Augustus is certainly a stronger candidate, as he offers a much better parallel for the title. But the messianic interpretation of 4Q246 is more plausible. All arguments that take the Son of God as a pagan king depend on the assumption that the *vacat* in column 2 marks a single turning point in the text. I find this assumption simplistic. Apocalyptic texts are seldom so simply constructed. In Daniel 12, for example, the rise of Michael is followed by a unique time of distress—and only then by the resurrection. The medieval chapter division was inserted on the assumption that the rise of Michael is a decisive turning point, as indeed it is, but an inference that everything from that point forward is positive would be clearly wrong. If we recognize that the *vacat* does not require a negative interpretation of the Son of God figure, then we must recognize that by far the closest parallel to the terminology is in the Gospel of Luke, where it is said that "the Lord God will give to him [the Son of God] the throne of David his father." Luke did not invent the messianic sense of "Son of God"—it was important for him that Jesus be identified with an established Jewish title. Besides, there is really no indication in 4Q246 (unlike the passage in Lactantius) that the title Son of God is inappropriate for the figure in question.

Nonetheless, Israel Knohl renders a service in drawing attention to the Roman connotation of "Son of God." While the title had old roots in the Hebrew Bible, it was not widely used in messianic texts around the turn of the era. It may be that the revival of "Son of God" as a messianic title was a reaction to the proclamation of Augustus as *divi filius*. The significance of emperor worship for both Jewish messianism and Christology is a subject that requires further study, as William Horbury argues.[4] The chief merit of Israel Knohl's book, in my opinion, is that it brings into the discussion the Roman context and neglected texts, like the *Oracle of Hystaspes*. I hope that we will have fruitful discussion of this material in the coming years.

4. William Horbury, *Jewish Messianism and the Cult of Christ* (London: SCM, 1998).

3

JESUS, JOHN, AND THE DEAD SEA SCROLLS

ASSESSING TYPOLOGIES OF RESTORATION

Craig A. Evans

At many points the Dead Sea Scrolls shed light on the world of Jesus and John, inaugurators of the movement that eventually became known as Christianity. One could approach this topic from several angles. One could examine the points of agreement in the use of Scripture: that is, which books and which specific passages are cited and how they are interpreted. One could examine the similarities in community structure and rules of membership, including discipline, disposal of personal property, and ritual requirements. One could compare the similarities in the understanding of the law of Moses. One could even compare the similarities in criticism leveled against outsiders and enemies. And of course, one could investigate the messianic ideas of Jesus, John, and the Dead Sea Scrolls. We could also mention some of the many studies that find several specific points of overlap between John and the Dead Sea Scrolls or between Jesus and the Dead Sea Scrolls. There are many, and they are significant.[1]

1. Two of the most current and accessible for nonexperts are C. M. Pate, *Communities of the Last Days: The Dead Sea Scrolls, the New Testament, and the Story*

45

The burden of the present essay, however, is to look for significant common ground of a typological nature. Our goal is to see how much light each can shed on the other: the scrolls on John, John on Jesus, the scrolls on Jesus, and—in reverse—the light that John and Jesus shed on the scrolls. What we shall find is a complex of typology that John, Jesus, and the scrolls community hold in common. Without necessarily arguing for direct contact or influence, we shall find a shared worldview, which includes a set of assumptions, a common sacred tradition, and overlapping hopes and goals.

These hopes and goals focus on the restoration of Israel, the people of God. This hope primarily concerns the Jewish people, but not necessarily to the exclusion of all other peoples. In the cases of John, Jesus, and the scrolls community, this restoration hope clarifies itself by invoking a wilderness typology, a water immersion typology, and a typology of the number twelve. There are other typologies to be sure, but I limit myself to these three in the confines of the present study.[2] The wilderness constitutes the setting, immersion constitutes the action, and the number twelve constitutes the goal. These points will become clear as we proceed.

Wilderness Typology

A cursory reading of the Bible reveals the symbolic value that the wilderness often has.[3] It is in the wilderness that Moses meets

---

of Israel (Downers Grove, IL: InterVarsity, 2000); and J. C. VanderKam and P. W. Flint, *The Meaning of the Dead Sea Scrolls: Their Significance for Understanding the Bible, Judaism, Jesus, and Christianity* (San Francisco: HarperCollins, 2002).

2. Other typologies well represented in the scrolls and in early Christian literature include the new covenant and the hope of a new Jerusalem. The former idea undergirds the respective movements' very self-understanding, while the latter gives expression to an important aspect of eschatology. On the general topic, see L. Goppelt, *Typos: The Typological Interpretation of the Old Testament in the New* (Grand Rapids: Eerdmans, 1982).

3. For summaries, see S. Talmon, "The 'Desert Motif' in the Bible and Qumran Literature," in *Biblical Motifs: Origins and Transformations* (ed. A. Altmann; Cambridge: Harvard University Press, 1966), 31–63; R. E. Watts, "Wilderness," in *New Dictionary of Biblical Theology* (ed. T. D. Alexander and B. S. Rosner; Leicester: Inter-Varsity, 2000), 841–43; D. W. Baker, "Wilderness, Desert," in *Dictionary*

God in the burning bush (Exod. 3:1–12). It is to the wilderness that God summons his people to worship him with sacrifice (3:18). In fact, Moses declares to Pharaoh: "Thus says the LORD, the God of Israel, 'Let my people go, that they may hold a feast to me in the wilderness'" (5:1). It is in the wilderness that the people of Israel witness the glory of the Lord (16:10). In the wilderness the Lord gives the people manna (16:14, 32: "I fed you in the wilderness"; cf. Deut. 8:16: "who fed you in the wilderness with manna"). Provisions of manna, meat, and water are among the signs that God worked in behalf of Israel in the wilderness (Num. 14:22). Indeed, God sustained Israel in the wilderness for forty years. The people lacked nothing; not even their shoes and clothes wore out (Deut. 29:5 [29:4 Heb.]; Neh. 9:21).

The wilderness wanderings of the people of Israel became the template on which later scriptural themes and typologies would be based. In Israel's history the wilderness was sometimes a place of refuge and hiding. We see this in the life of David, especially when evading the wrathful Benjamite king, Saul (1 Sam. 23:14). Indeed, David was sometimes in the vicinity of En-gedi, near the Dead Sea (24:1 [24:2 Heb.]), not far from Qumran and the nearby caves in which the ancient scrolls would be found many centuries later. During a period of religious and political apostasy, the prophet Elijah fled into the wilderness to escape Ahab and Jezebel. There he too found his needs provided for (1 Kings 19:1–8; cf. 17:1–6).

The exodus, the giving of the covenant, and the signs and wonders performed in the wilderness became themes in later

---

of the Old Testament: Pentateuch (ed. T. D. Alexander and D. W. Baker; Downers Grove, IL: InterVarsity, 2003), 893–97; and W. Brueggemann, *Reverberations of Faith: A Theological Handbook of Old Testament Themes* (Louisville: Westminster John Knox, 2002), 72–75. For a sampling of recent studies, see T. B. Dozeman, "Geography and Ideology in the Wilderness Journey from Kadesh through the Transjordan," in *Abschied vom Jahwisten: Die Komposition des Hexateuch in der jüngsten Diskussion* (ed. J. C. Gertz et al.; Beihefte zur Zeitschrift für die alttestamentliche Wissenschaft 315; Berlin/New York: de Gruyter, 2002), 173–89; idem, "The Wilderness and Salvation History in the Hagar Story," *Journal of Biblical Literature* 117 (1998): 23–43; D. Frankel, "Two Priestly Conceptions of Guidance in the Wilderness," *Journal for the Study of the Old Testament* 81 (1998): 31–37; P. D. Miller, *Israelite Religion and Biblical Theology: Collected Essays* (Journal for the Study of the Old Testament Supplement 267; Sheffield: JSOT Press, 2000), 572–92.

scriptural traditions, especially in the Psalter. Psalms 77, 78, and 136 are especially noteworthy. Psalms 77 and 136 dwell upon the positive dimension of the tradition, recalling the crossing of the divided sea (77:15–19 [77:16–20 Heb.]; 136:12–15) and divine leading in the wilderness (77:20 [77:21 Heb.]; 136:16–18). Psalm 78 reminds Israel of its forgetfulness and unbelief, despite the many wonders (78:11–29). God worked marvels in Egypt, divided the sea, led the people in the wilderness with the pillar of fire and of cloud, provided water, bread, meat—yet they did not remember. The theme of obduracy is expressed in the Mosaic narrative itself, where the long-suffering Moses reminds Israel that despite God's signs wrought before them, the people continually tested God (Num. 14:22; Deut. 29:2–4 [29:1–3 Heb.]).

Exodus typology plays a very important role in the book of Isaiah.[4] Sea and wilderness are the key referents. In an oracle against Assyria, the prophet encourages Israel that its enemy will be struck down the way the Egyptians were (Isa. 10:24–27). God's "rod will be over the sea, and he will lift it as he did in Egypt" (10:26). The day will come when God will gather his scattered people from the nations that oppress Israel (11:10–16). On that day the "LORD will utterly destroy the tongue of the sea of Egypt; and will wave his hand over the River [Euphrates] with his scorching wind, and smite it into seven channels that men may cross dryshod" (11:15). The result will be a "highway from Assyria" for Israel's remnant, just as there had been when God delivered his people from Egypt (11:16).

The whole of Isaiah 35 revolves around the theme of restoration, beginning with the blossoming of the wilderness (35:1–2). It will be a day of salvation, when God will save (35:4), when the "eyes of the blind will be opened, and the ears of the deaf unstopped; then shall the lame man leap like a hart, and the tongue of the dumb sing for joy" (35:5–6a). As it was in the days of the wilderness wanderings, so in the period of restoration: "Waters shall break forth in the wilderness, and streams in the

4. See the summaries in B. W. Anderson, "Exodus Typology in Second Isaiah," in *Israel's Prophetic Heritage: Essays in Honor of James Muilenburg* (ed. B. W. Anderson and W. Harrelson; New York: Harper, 1962), 177–95; J. Blenkinsopp, *Isaiah 1–39* (Anchor Bible 19; New York: Doubleday, 2000), 268; idem, *Isaiah 40–55* (Anchor Bible 19A; New York: Doubleday, 2002), 111–12.

desert" (35:6b). And, as we have already seen, God will provide a highway, on which the redeemed of the Lord will return to Zion rejoicing (35:8–10).

Running throughout the oracles of comfort and renewal in Isaiah 40–44 are allusions to the wilderness sojourn and God's provision for his people. The prophet hears a voice cry: "In the wilderness prepare the way of the Lord, make straight in the desert a highway for our God. Every valley shall be lifted up, and every mountain and hill be made low; the uneven ground shall become level, and the rough places a plain" (40:3–5). Just as God provided a highway through the sea, so now he will provide a highway from Babylon to Israel, so that the exiles may return home. As of old, God will again provide water in the wilderness: "I will open rivers on the bare heights, and fountains in the middle of the valleys; I will make the wilderness a pool of water, and the dry land springs of water" (41:18). The desert wilderness will become fruitful, a place of forest (41:19). The Lord will lead his people, though they be blind, and level the rugged places before them (42:16).

The oracle in Isaiah 43:14–21 makes explicit the comparison between the return from the Babylonian exile and the original exodus from Egypt: "For your sake I will send to Babylon and break down all the bars, and the shouting of the Chaldeans will be turned to lamentations. . . . Thus says the Lord, who makes a way in the sea, a path in the mighty waters, who brings forth chariot and horse, army and warrior; they lie down, they cannot rise, they are extinguished" (43:14–17). What God is doing is so special that he tells his people to forget about the past: "Remember not the former things, nor consider the things of old" (43:18). "Behold, I am doing a new thing; now it springs forth, do you not perceive it? I will make a way in the wilderness and rivers in the desert" (43:19).

Restoration through the provision of water in the wilderness, in Isaiah 44, is likened to the pouring out of God's Spirit: "I will pour water on the thirsty land, and streams on the dry ground; I will pour my Spirit upon your descendants, and my blessing on your offspring" (44:3). This concept is echoed again later in the Isaianic collection, where we are told that God (or his people—the Hebrew is uncertain) "remembered the days of old, of Moses his servant. Where is he who brought up out of the sea the shepherds of his flock? Where is he who put in the middle of them his holy Spirit?" (63:11).

The imagery of a watered and fructified desert appears again in Isaiah: "For the Lord will comfort Zion; he will comfort all her waste places and will make her wilderness like Eden, her desert like the garden of the Lord; joy and gladness will be found in her, thanksgiving and the voice of song" (51:3).

God reminds Israel that he is more than powerful enough to save, reminding his people of when he dried up the sea (50:2; cf. 19:5–6). With this image in mind, the prophet cries out to God to arm himself, asking: "Was it not you who dried up the sea, the waters of the great deep; who made the depths of the sea a way for the redeemed to pass over?" (51:10).

The image of wilderness wandering is well attested elsewhere in Scripture and in the intertestamental literature also (e.g., Jer. 2:1–6; Ezek. 20:10; Hos. 11:1; 13:4–5; Amos 2:10; 5:25; Ps. 68:7–8 [68:8–9 Heb.]; 78:13–16; 136:10–22; Jdt. 5:14; Wis. 11:2; 2 Esd. [= 4 Ezra] 9:29; 1 Enoch 89.28; Testament of Moses 3.11).

We should hardly be surprised that the restoration movements in Israel in late antiquity appealed to such rich imagery and time-honored sacred tradition. The Essenes (who are the most probable custodians of that ancient library we call the Dead Sea Scrolls), John the Baptist, Jesus, and other figures, such as Theudas, mentioned in the book of Acts and in Josephus, are among the best-known figures, whose movements were in some way linked with the wilderness typology.

In the *Community Rule*, one of the most important scrolls, we have explicit appeal to Isaiah 40:3:

> When such men as these come to be in Israel, conforming to these doctrines, they shall separate from the session of perverse men to go to the wilderness, there to prepare the way of truth, as it is written, "In the wilderness prepare the way of the Lord, make straight in the desert a highway for our God" (Isa. 40:3). This means the expounding of the law, decreed by God through Moses for obedience, that being defined by what has been revealed for each age, and by what the prophets have revealed by His holy spirit. (1QS 8.12b–16a)[5]

5. Translations of the Dead Sea Scrolls are based on M. O. Wise, M. G. Abegg Jr., and E. M. Cook, *The Dead Sea Scrolls: A New Translation* (San Francisco: HarperCollins, 1996).

Interpretation of Isaiah 40:3 is both literal and metaphorical. Its literal interpretation is seen in the community's location in the wilderness near the Dead Sea, and its metaphorical interpretation is seen in understanding the "Way" as a reference to the community itself. This metaphorical nuance is seen a little later in the *Community Rule*:

> He shall save reproof—itself founded on true knowledge and righteous judgment—for those who have chosen the Way, treating each as his spiritual qualities and the precepts of the era require. He shall ground them in knowledge, thereby instructing them in truly wondrous mysteries; if then the secret Way is perfected among the men of the Community, each will walk blamelessly with his fellow, guided by what has been revealed to them. That will be the time of "preparing the way in the desert" (Isa. 40:3). He shall instruct them in every legal finding that is to regulate their works in that time, and teach them to separate from every man who fails to keep himself from perversity.
>
> These are the precepts of the Way for the Instructor in these times, as to his loving and hating: eternal hatred and a concealing spirit for the Men of the Pit! (1QS 9.17b–22a)[6]

The parallel with Christian origins is remarkable and has not gone unobserved.[7] Not only was Isaiah 40:3 associated with

---

6. On the importance of Isa. 40:3 at Qumran, see G. J. Brooke, "Isaiah 40:3 and the Wilderness Community," in *New Qumran Texts and Studies: Proceedings of the First Meeting of the International Organization for Qumran Studies, Paris 1992* (ed. G. J. Brooke and F. García Martínez; Studies on the Texts of the Desert of Judah 15; Leiden: Brill, 1994), 117–32; J. H. Charlesworth, "Intertextuality: Isaiah 40:3 and the Serek ha-Yaḥad," in *The Quest for Context and Meaning: Studies in Biblical Intertextuality in Honor of James A. Sanders* (ed. C. A. Evans and S. Talmon; Biblical Interpretation Series 28; Leiden: Brill, 1997), 197–224.

7. See the classic discussion by U. Mauser, *Christ in the Wilderness: The Wilderness Theme in the Second Gospel and Its Basis in the Biblical Tradition* (Studies in Biblical Theology 1/39; London: SCM/Naperville: Allenson, 1963). More recent studies include K. R. Snodgrass, "Streams of Tradition Emerging from Isaiah 40.1–5 and Their Adaptation in the New Testament," in *New Testament Backgrounds: A Sheffield Reader* (ed. C. A. Evans and S. E. Porter; Biblical Seminar 43; Sheffield: Sheffield Academic Press, 1997), 149–68; B. W. Longenecker, "The Wilderness and Revolutionary Ferment in First-Century Palestine: A Response to D. R. Schwartz and J. Marcus," *Journal for the Study of Judaism in the Persian, Hellenistic, and Roman Period* 29 (1998): 322–36; B. J. Oropeza, "Apostasy in the Wilderness: Paul's Message to the Corinthians in a State of Eschatological Lim-

John the Baptist, who appeared in the wilderness preaching repentance, but the early Christian movement, like the Essene community, referred to itself as the Way (cf. Acts 9:2; 19:9, 23; 24:14, 22).

Other parallels notwithstanding, in my view it is unnecessary to suppose a direct link between early Christianity and the men of Qumran, the Essenes. I say this not only because of the profound systemic differences between the two movements,[8] but because of evidence that the typology of wilderness as place of restoration was widespread. Postulating direct lines of influence creates more problems than it solves.

One example of a wilderness prophet of restoration, of whom we know some details, is Theudas. The author of the book of Acts knows of him, saying through Gamaliel the Pharisee, "For before these days Theudas arose, giving himself out to be somebody, and a number of men, about four hundred, joined him; but he was slain and all who followed him were dispersed and came to nothing" (Acts 5:36). Josephus provides us with a far more helpful discussion of this man:

> Now it came to pass, while Fadus was procurator of Judea, that a certain impostor, whose name was Theudas, persuaded a great part of the people to take their effects with them, and follow him to the river Jordan; for he told them he was a prophet and that he would, by his own command, divide the river and afford them an easy passage over it; and many were deluded by his words. However, Fadus did not permit them to make any advantage of his wild attempt, but sent a troop of horsemen out against them; who, falling upon them unexpectedly, slew many of them and took many of them alive. They also took Theudas alive and cut off his head and carried it to Jerusalem. (*Antiquities* 20.97–98)[9]

inality," *Journal for the Study of the New Testament* 75 (1999): 69–86; J. Schwartz, "John the Baptist, the Wilderness, and the Samaritan Mission," in *Studies in Historical Geography and Biblical Historiography* (ed. G. Galil and M. Weinfeld; Vetus Testamentum Supplement 81; Leiden: Brill, 2000), 104–17.

8. See C. A. Evans, "Comparing Judaisms: Qumranic, Rabbinic, and Jacobean Judaisms Compared," in *The Brother of Jesus: James the Just and His Mission* (ed. B. D. Chilton and J. Neusner; Louisville: Westminster John Knox, 2001), 161–83.

9. Translations of Josephus are based on W. A. M. Whiston, *The Genuine Works of Flavius Josephus, the Jewish Historian: Translated from the Original Greek,*

It is almost certain that the biblical story of the wilderness sojourn and especially of the crossing of the Jordan River provided the scriptural typology for Theudas and his following. Like Joshua of old (cf. Josh. 4), the successor of Moses, the latter-day prophet believed he could part the Jordan. Those who followed him to the Jordan carried with them their personal effects, just as did the wilderness generation. The implication is clear: the parting of the Jordan would signify that God was leading the way into the promised land, as a new conquest and a new beginning.

The appearance of John the Baptist in the wilderness, at the Jordan River, is surely related to this typology.[10] Jesus's baptism by John (Matt. 3:13; Mark 1:9; Luke 3:21), his temptation in the wilderness (Matt. 4:1–11; Mark 1:12–13; Luke 4:1–13), and his multiplication of the loaves in the wilderness (Matt. 14:15–21; Mark 6:35–44; Luke 9:12–17; John 6:1–14) would have been interpreted by his followers in the light of this typology.

This is not to say that there were no significant differences between John the Baptist, Jesus, Theudas, and the men of the Dead Sea Scrolls. Theirs was a shared typology, broadly speaking, but it was a typology capable of differing interpretation and application. Some of these differences will become clear in the next two typologies.

Immersion Typology

Ritual immersion in water for purification purposes is taught in the Mosaic law (e.g., Lev. 11–15). In New Testament times most Jewish homes were furnished with a *miqveh* (lit., "gathering of water"; plural *miqvaoth*) that facilitated the requirements of ritual

---

according to Havercamp's Accurate Edition (London: Bowyer, 1737; subsequently reprinted many times); and the Thackeray-Marcus-Wikgren-Feldman translation in the Loeb Classical Library (*Josephus: Works* [trans. H. St. J. Thackeray, Ralph Marcus, Allen Wikgren, and L. H. Feldman; 13 vols.; Cambridge: Harvard University Press; London: Heinemann, 1926–65]).

10. See C. A. Evans, "The Baptism of John in a Typological Context," in *Dimensions of Baptism: Biblical and Theological Studies* (ed. A. R. Cross and S. E. Porter; Journal for the Study of the New Testament Supplement 234; Sheffield: Sheffield Academic Press, 2002), 45–71.

bathing. Excavations in the Jewish quarter of Jerusalem and at Sepphoris in Galilee reveal a number of examples.[11]

In the ruins of Qumran six *miqvaoth* have been identified (though there is some debate on this point).[12] These *miqvaoth* have steps and are divided in the middle in order to separate the impure person who descends from the pure person who ascends (cf. Mishnah, tractate *Sheqalim* 8.2). Qumran's *miqvaoth* are much larger than those found in homes in Jerusalem, Jericho, and other locations in Israel, probably attesting to the larger, communal population of Essenes.

The Dead Sea Scrolls themselves contain statements that attest the community's interest in ritual immersion. According to the *Community Rule*:

> None of the perverse men is to enter purifying waters used by the Men of Holiness and so contact their purity. (Indeed, it is impossible to be purified without first repenting of evil, inasmuch as impurity adheres to all who transgress his word.) None is to be yoked with such a man in his work or wealth, lest "he cause him to bear guilt" [Lev. 22:16]. On the contrary, one must keep far from him in every respect, for thus it is written: "Keep far from every false thing" [Exod. 23:7]. None belonging to the community is to discuss with such men matters of law or legal judgment, nor to eat or drink what is theirs, nor yet to take anything from them unless purchased, as it is written, "Turn away from mere mortals, in whose nostrils is only breath; for of what account are they?" [Isa. 2:22]. Accordingly, all who are not reckoned as belonging to his covenant must be separated out. (1QS 5.13–18)

The reference to "perverse men" entering "purifying waters" almost certainly refers to the community's practice of ritual im-

11. E. M. Meyers, "Yes, They Are," *Biblical Archaeology Review* 26.4 (2000): 46–49, 60; and M. A. Chancey, *The Myth of a Gentile Galilee* (Society for New Testament Study Monograph 118; Cambridge: Cambridge University Press, 2002), 79–81. Meyers writes in response to H. Eshel's "They Are Not Ritual Baths," *Biblical Archaeology Review* 26.4 (2000): 42–45, who expresses reservations about the identifications of the *miqvaoth* at Sepphoris.

12. See the summary of the evidence in R. Reich, "*Miqva'ot*," in *Encyclopedia of the Dead Sea Scrolls* (ed. L. H. Schiffman and J. C. VanderKam; Oxford: Oxford University Press, 2000), 1:560–63; and J. Magness, *The Archaeology of Qumran and the Dead Sea Scrolls* (Studies in the Dead Sea Scrolls and Related Literature; Grand Rapids: Eerdmans, 2002), 134–62.

mersion and, in the context of Qumran itself, to the *miqvaoth* uncovered in the excavations of the ruins. The desire to avoid contact of pure with impure, as witnessed by the barriers that divide the steps in the *miqvaoth*, coheres with the community's intense desire to shun those they regard as perverse and impure. No member of the community is to be "yoked" with such a person or his wealth. Indeed, members of the community are to "keep far from every false thing" (quoting Exod. 23:7). Members of the Essene community are not to discuss their understanding of the law with outsiders, nor are they "to eat or drink what is theirs." If they do not belong to God's covenant, they "must be separated out."

We find important coherence with John the Baptist. According to Josephus, John

> was a good man and commanded the Jews to exercise virtue, both as to righteousness toward one another and piety toward God, and so to come to baptism; for that the washing [with water] would be acceptable to him, if they made use of it, not for the putting away [or the remission] of some sins [only], but for the purification of the body; supposing still that the soul was thoroughly purified beforehand by righteousness. Now, when [many] others came in crowds about him, for they were greatly moved [or pleased] by hearing his words, Herod became alarmed. (*Antiquities* 18.117–18)

Also, according to the Gospels John warned those who approached him:

> You brood of vipers! Who warned you to flee from the wrath to come? Bear fruit that befits repentance, and do not presume to say to yourselves, "We have Abraham as our father"; for I tell you, God is able from these stones to raise up children to Abraham. Even now the axe is laid to the root of the trees; every tree therefore that does not bear good fruit is cut down and thrown into the fire. (Matt. 3:7–10)

John's explicit rejection of descent from Abraham indicates that he does not regard these people as part of the people of God. His language is hardly less severe than what we find in the Dead Sea Scrolls. Before these people can be called "children of

Abraham," they must "bear fruit that befits repentance." This requirement essentially agrees with the description in Josephus, in which we are told that John commanded fellow Jews to "exercise virtue" and that "washing" was valid only if accompanied by "righteousness toward one another and piety toward God." This is not much different from John's advice found in Luke, where he commands the people to share with those in need and the officers not to cheat or extort (Luke 3:10–14).

The notion that outer washing is of no value if not accompanied by repentance and righteousness is attested in the teaching of Jesus as well. It is implicit in his debate with Pharisees over what really defiles (Mark 7:1–23). It is not what goes into a person, but what comes out of his heart (7:14–15; cf. 1 Sam. 16:7: "Man looks on the outward appearance, but the LORD looks on the heart"). It is implicit in the antitheses of the Sermon on the Mount (e.g., Matt. 5:21–30) and is given vigorous expression in what is probably an apocryphal story found in an Egyptian papyrus. In response to a Pharisaic priest who had criticized Jesus and his disciples as unwashed and therefore unfit for viewing the sacred vessels in the temple, an angry Jesus retorts:

> Woe, you blind who do not see. You have washed in these running waters in which dogs and swine have [been] cast night and day, and have cleaned and wiped the outside skin which also the harlots and flute-girls anoint and wash and wipe and beautify for the lust of men; but within they are full of scorpions and all wickedness. But I and my disciples, who you say have not bathed, have been dipped in the waters of eternal life. (P.Oxy. 840, with some restoration)[13]

The story may well be a fiction (as most scholars think), but it probably fairly represents the mind of Jesus on this matter.

Finally, we should note that the typology of crossing the sea and baptism come together in Paul:

> I want you to know, brethren, that our fathers were all under the cloud, and all passed through the sea, and all were baptized into Moses in the cloud and in the sea, and all ate the same supernatural

13. Cf. B. P. Grenfell and A. S. Hunt, eds., *The Oxyrhynchus Papyri*, vol. 5 (London: Egypt Exploration Fund, 1908), no. 840.

food and all drank the same supernatural drink. For they drank from the supernatural rock which followed them, and the rock was Christ. Nevertheless, with most of them God was not pleased; for they were overthrown in the wilderness. (1 Cor. 10:1–5)

A measure of innovation cannot be ruled out. However, it is probable that most of this typology reflects pre-Pauline Christianizing of the older Jewish traditions that grew out of the exodus and wilderness stories.[14] What is important to underscore is the association of wilderness and crossing the water. Both evoke powerful images of God's saving activity.

Twelve Typology

According to John, baptism, accompanied by repentance and commitment to righteousness, leads to covenant renewal. The number twelve plays an important role in the typologies of wilderness and baptism. The typology of twelve signifies the renewal of the whole of Israel, that is, all twelve tribes. Before we return to John, Jesus, and the Dead Sea Scrolls, a review of the biblical data will be helpful.[15]

The number twelve gains its significance from the number of Jacob's sons: "Now the sons of Jacob were twelve" (Gen. 35:22). The twelve sons, with minor adjustments involving Joseph and his sons, become the patriarchs of the twelve tribes of Israel (49:28). The twelveness of Israel's composition was expressed in a variety of symbols. Moses builds an altar at the foot of Mount Sinai, with "twelve pillars, according to the twelve tribes of Israel" (Exod. 24:4). On the priestly breastplate there "shall be twelve stones with their names according to the names of the sons of Israel; they shall be like signets, each engraved with its name, for the twelve tribes" (28:21; cf. 39:14; *Letter of Aristeas* 97).

14. Paul's interesting statement that the rock "followed" the Israelites coheres with targumic and midrashic tradition; cf. *Targum Neofiti* Num. 21:17–19; Tosefta, tractate *Sukkah* 3.11.

15. See the summary on "Twelve," in *Dictionary of Biblical Imagery* (ed. L. Ryken et al.; Downers Grove, IL: InterVarsity, 1998), 900–901. See also S. Freyne, *The Twelve: Disciples and Apostles: A Study in the Theology of the First Three Gospels* (London: Sheed & Ward, 1968).

The symbolism of the number twelve is reinforced in the conquest of the promised land. In preparation for the crossing of the Jordan River, Joshua commands the people: "Now therefore take twelve men from the tribes of Israel, from each tribe a man" (Josh. 3:12; cf. 4:2). After crossing the Jordan, Joshua issues another command: "Take twelve stones from here out of the middle of the Jordan, from the very place where the priests' feet stood, and carry them over with you, and lay them down in the place where you lodge tonight" (4:3; cf. 4:8).

The men do as Joshua ordered them. Joshua then takes the twelve stones and places them "where the feet of the priests bearing the ark of the covenant had stood; and they are there to this day" (Josh. 4:9). Joshua goes on to instruct Israel:

> When your children ask their fathers in time to come, "What do these stones mean?" then you shall let your children know, "Israel passed over this Jordan on dry ground." For the LORD your God dried up the waters of the Jordan for you until you passed over, as the LORD your God did to the Red Sea, which he dried up for us until we passed over, so that all the peoples of the earth may know that the hand of the LORD is mighty; that you may fear the LORD your God forever. (Josh. 4:21–24)

The symbolism of the twelve stones comes into play during the later period of apostasy under Ahab and Jezebel. One recalls the famous contest between Elijah and the prophets of Baal at Mount Carmel. In the presence of Israel "Elijah took twelve stones, according to the number of the tribes of the sons of Jacob, to whom the word of the LORD came, saying, 'Israel shall be your name' [cf. Gen. 32:28 (32:29 Heb.)]; and with the stones he built an altar in the name of the LORD" (1 Kings 18:31–32). Elsewhere in the prophetic tradition, hope for the restoration of the twelve tribes is expressed (e.g., Isa. 49:6; 63:17; Ezek. 37:19; 45:8; 47:13; and *Psalms of Solomon* 17.26, 28, where this hope is expressly messianic and Davidic).[16]

16. In the much later rabbinic tradition there is debate whether the ten northern tribes will in fact be restored; cf. Mishnah, tractate *Sanhedrin* 10.3: "Rabbi Eliezer says, 'Concerning them it says, "The Lord kills and resurrects, brings down to Sheol and brings up again" [1 Sam. 2:6].' The ten tribes are not destined to return, since it is said, "And he cast them into another land, as on this day" [Deut. 29:28 (29:27 Heb.)]. Just as the day passes and does not return, so they

The typology of twelve finds expression in the Dead Sea Scrolls. We see it in the structure and order of the community: "In the council of the community there shall be twelve laymen and three priests who are blameless in the light of all that has been revealed" (1QS 8.1). The order for battle, as outlined in the *War Scroll*, includes twelve ruling priests and twelve chiefs of the Levites (1QM 2.1–2 = 4Q494 4–5; cf. 4Q164 frag. 1 line 4). The names of the twelve tribes are to be written on the banners that will be carried into battle (1QM 3.13–14) and on the shield of the prince of the whole congregation, that is, the messiah (1QM 5.1–2).

Other passages from Scripture, cited above, that mention twelve tribes or twelve priests are quoted or alluded to in other scrolls (e.g., 4Q158 frag. 4 lines 2–3; 4Q364 frag. 21 line 12; 4Q365 frag. 12b 3.12–13; frag. 35 2.4; 4Q379 frag. 1 line 5; 4Q471 frag. 1 lines 2–5). In another scroll we find reference to "ten laymen and two priests," before whom the wicked are to be judged: "and they shall be judged before these twelve" (4Q159 frags. 2–4 lines 3–4). One immediately recalls the words of Jesus to his disciples: "Truly, I say to you, in the new world, when the Son of Man shall sit on his glorious throne, you who have followed me will also sit on twelve thrones, judging the twelve tribes of Israel" (Matt. 19:28; cf. Luke 22:28–30).

In the New Testament passage just cited, to which we shall return shortly, we find mention of twelve thrones and twelve tribes. Implicit, of course, are the twelve apostles who will sit on these twelve thrones. The twelve apostles are well known. Why did Jesus appoint twelve?

Most interpreters rightly assume that the twelve disciples—later apostles—were meant to represent the twelve tribes of Israel. Their proclamation of repentance and the presence of the kingdom of God surely implied the restoration of the whole of Israel—all twelve tribes. In view of the scriptural and postscriptural traditions reviewed above, Jesus's use of this symbol, as part of a biblical typology of restoration, can hardly surprise.[17]

---

have gone their way and will not return,' the words of Rabbi Aqiba. Rabbi Eliezer says, 'Just as this day is dark and then grows light, so the ten tribes for whom it now is dark—thus in the future it is destined to grow light for them.'"

17. See W. Horbury, "The Twelve and the Phylarchs," *New Testament Studies* 32 (1986): 503–27; and S. McKnight, "Jesus and the Twelve," *Bulletin for Biblical Research* 11 (2001): 203–31.

His contemporaries would have readily understood its import. Is the twelve typology in Jesus's teaching and activities linked in any way to his colleague John the Baptist? I believe it is.

Admittedly, the number twelve does not appear on the lips of John, either in the New Testament Gospels or in Josephus. But twelve typology may well lie behind his scathing criticism: "You brood of vipers! Who warned you to flee from the wrath to come? Bear fruit that befits repentance, and do not presume to say to yourselves, 'We have Abraham as our father'; for I tell you, God is able from these stones to raise up children to Abraham" (Matt. 3:7–9 = Luke 3:7–8).

To what do John's words "these stones" refer? The phrase "these stones" occurs four times in the Hebrew Bible—three of them referring to the twelve stones that Joshua ordered set up after the crossing of the Jordan River (Josh. 4:7, 21; cf. Deut. 27:4). It is probable that John, baptizing in the Jordan and preaching a message that was to prepare Israel for coming salvation, a message related to or in fulfillment of Isaiah 40, had set up—like Joshua of old—a memorial made of twelve stones representing the twelve tribes of Israel. This interpretation makes sense of his warning not to say, "We have Abraham as our father." Their descent from Abraham means nothing, for God can raise up sons of the twelve stones, that is, the twelve tribes. The memorial of the twelve stones was intended to remind the descendants of the wilderness generation that it was the Lord who brought Israel across the Jordan and into the promised land—something, from John's point of view, that his generation had forgotten.

Accordingly, Jesus's appointment of the twelve (Mark 3:14; 6:7) is an extension of John's typology.[18] The Jordan River has been crossed, and now representatives of the restored tribes have reentered the promised land, announcing the rule of God. If the nation repents, restoration will take place. It will be a time when the twelve apostles will sit on twelve thrones, judging the twelve tribes of Israel, judging not in a condemning sense but in an administrative, even shepherding sense.[19]

That the earliest Christian movement thought of itself as a restoration movement within Israel is quite clear and is attested

18. For more detailed argument, see my "Baptism of John," 68–70.
19. As the judges in the book of Judges and as in 4Q159, cited above.

in the letter of James, which is addressed "to the twelve tribes in the Dispersion" (James 1:1), or in 1 Peter, whose author speaks of his addressees as "the exiles of the Dispersion" (1 Pet. 1:1). The hope of the restoration of the twelve tribes of Israel is strong in Christianity's first generation, though in time it fades. This early hope is attested in the Paul of Acts, who declares before King Agrippa: "And now I stand here on trial for hope in the promise made by God to our fathers, to which our twelve tribes hope to attain, as they earnestly worship night and day. And for this hope I am accused by Jews, O king!" (Acts 26:6–7). To be sure, in this context Paul refers to the resurrection hope, but this nevertheless remains a dimension of the hope of the restoration of the twelve tribes.

Conclusion

The burden of the present study was to clarify the extent to which the early Christian movement understood itself in terms of biblical typology that gave expression to hopes of the restoration of Israel. It is significant that the origins of the movement, beginning with John the Baptist, were rooted in wilderness typology, an important dimension that overlapped with ideas found in the Dead Sea Scrolls.

Perhaps more surprising to Christians is how deeply rooted in Jewish Scripture and tradition other important and related typologies are. These include ritual immersion and the number twelve. The latter has atrophied in the subsequent history of Christian theology and practice, though traces of it remain (e.g., in the form of twelve elders or deacons on the board of the local church). The former has perdured, though not without important changes in how it is understood.

In John immersion was as much purificatory as it was eschatological. This stands in continuity with Mosaic legislation, later Jewish custom, and ideas and practices attested in the Dead Sea Scrolls and in the architectural remains that their authors left behind at Qumran.

It is not surprising that, given the early church's eschatological orientation and its evolution toward an increasingly Gentile membership, the dimension of baptism that eclipsed all other forms and meanings was the baptism that signified entry into the community of faith. Initiatory, once-only baptism became Christianity's only point of reference and so became the lens through which the baptizing activity of John, Jesus, and their disciples has been often viewed.

We find that the very structure of the early Christian community grows out of a typology (or set of typologies) rooted in the sacred Scriptures of Israel. This structure cannot be adequately understood without a careful and nuanced appreciation of the Dead Sea Scrolls.

4

PAUL AND JAMES ON THE LAW IN LIGHT OF THE DEAD SEA SCROLLS

Martin G. Abegg Jr.

Interest in the Dead Sea Scrolls continues unabated since their discovery in the late 1940s and early 1950s. We sense that they contain wonderful treasure. And they do. They do not answer all the tough questions, but they do provide important background to the world of the Jewish writers who penned the New Testament and the ancient rabbis who gathered the materials that provide the foundations for modern Judaism. As Shemaryahu Talmon writes: "The scrolls promise to give some help for partly inscribing the proverbial blank page between the Hebrew Bible and the Mishnah on the one hand, and between the Hebrew Bible and the New Testament on the other hand."[1]

Identifying these links is the purpose of the present volume and the interest of each of the authors. I myself am frequently asked, often by reporters looking for the latest bit of controversy,

1. S. Talmon, "The Community of the Renewed Covenant, between Judaism and Christianity," in *The Community of the Renewed Covenant* (ed. E. Ulrich and J. C. VanderKam; Notre Dame: University of Notre Dame Press, 1994), 4.

what are the most significant discoveries in the scrolls? The topic of my study is foremost in my scholarly interest.

In 1988 a previously unpublished document began circulating among scroll scholars, often arriving in the proverbial "brown manila envelope," with no return address. This document was of obvious importance for both of Talmon's stated interests, and it was for this reason that in the spring following the receipt of this surreptitious mailing, Hebrew Union College listed in its graduate catalog the course Hellenistic Literature 25, taught by Ben Zion Wacholder. The course was devoted solely to a study of the document that was available at the time only in a photocopy of someone's handwritten notes. The handwritten notes thankfully proved to be bona fide, and from that time until now, this work, known now by its acronym, 4QMMT, which stands for *miqṣat ma'aśe ha-torah* ("some of the works of the law"), has never been far from my thinking and has taken its rightful place as one of the most important Dead Sea Scrolls.

It was fully five years later, in the fall of 1994, that I had the first opportunity to discuss my understanding of this scroll in print. In an article titled "Paul, Works of the Law, and the MMT,"[2] I concluded rather simply that the phrase *miqṣat ma'aśe ha-torah* (4QMMT C26–27) was the Hebrew equivalent to the expression "works of the law," found in the Apostle Paul's letters to the Galatians and Romans. In fact, the phrase occurs nowhere else in antiquity, apart from Paul's expression ἔργα νόμου—works of the law—in eight instances in these two missives (Rom. 3:20, 28; Gal. 2:16 [three times]; 3:2, 5, 10). Using the Septuagint for lexical confirmation, statistically and contextually the translation of מעשׂה ("work") by ἔργον and תורה ("law") by νόμος is a near certainty.

The works of the law to which our Dead Sea Scrolls writer refers are typified by the more than twenty-four precepts that are detailed in the main body of this text (4QMMT B1–C4). These concern, in the main, acts that trespass the boundaries between the pure and impure in the temple precincts. In my 1994 article I concluded that 4QMMT reveals that Paul was not simply "jousting with windmills" but was indeed squared off in a dramatic

---

2. M. G. Abegg Jr., "Paul, Works of the Law, and the MMT," *Biblical Archaeology Review* 20.6 (1994): 52–55.

duel that ultimately defined a form of messianic Judaism that became known as Christianity.

In a second article, in 1999, I began probing the significance of this parallelism.[3] I explored the possibility that I had been extravagant in my claims, perhaps exaggerating the points of contact, even to the point of being guilty of what Samuel Sandmel describes as "parallelomania."[4] Once again I investigated the significance of such common language. I began with the thesis that the Qumran manuscripts might now offer the opportunity of aiding our search for the type of Judaism with which Paul was interacting. In the main I simply underlined the conclusions of E. P. Sanders, who had pursued a similar course—albeit from the starting point of rabbinic literature—some twenty years before.[5] Sanders, with J. D. G. Dunn in his wake, was recognized as the chief founder of a "new perspective on Paul," an apt expression coined by Dunn in a 1983 study.[6] I entered this discussion through the back door, as it were, for even as late as 1994, focused as I was on Qumran texts, I was blissfully unaware of the significance of Dunn and Sanders for my own studies. I had come to the new perspective not as a follower of Dunn, but as a student of 4QMMT.

In relation to the Qumran manuscripts, this perspective posits that the sectarians who collected, copied, and perhaps in some cases even composed the scrolls believed that righteousness originated with God, not humans. The community entrance requirement—and thus right relationship with God—is clearly shown to be repentance of sin. A knee-jerk reaction that 4QMMT and the community literature as a whole reflect a "works earn righteousness" religion is hardly justified. Again to emphasize, entrance into the community was always couched in the language of repentance. Maintenance, once one was a member of the covenant, was on the basis of the member's understanding of the law

3. M. G. Abegg Jr., "4QMMT C27, 31 and 'Works Righteousness'?" *Dead Sea Discoveries* 6 (1999): 139–47.

4. S. Sandmel, "Parallelomania," *Journal of Biblical Literature* 81 (1962): 1–13.

5. E. P. Sanders, *Paul and Palestinian Judaism* (Philadelphia: Fortress, 1977).

6. J. D. G. Dunn, "The New Perspective on Paul," *Bulletin of the John Rylands University Library* 65 (1983): 95–103.

as interpreted by the community. Jews who refused to repent, as well as covenanters who subsequently rejected the restrictions of the law, were judged according to the law. Repentance was not possible for the Gentiles; they were judged in consonance with their evil deeds.

There does not appear to be any variation in any of the scrolls concerning this basic pattern. As Sanders writes: "The place of obedience [to the law] in the overall scheme is always the same: it is the *consequence* of being in the covenant and the *requirement for remaining in the covenant.*"[7] Nothing in the scrolls bolsters the Protestant teaching that Jews of antiquity would have considered themselves "saved" or, in other words, entering into a relationship with God on the basis of doing works of the law.

Thus to clarify the significance of the phrase "works of the law," we may describe this group this way: "they honor their parents, they do not murder, commit adultery, steal, or bear false witness." Apart from instantly recognizable biblical phrases such as "bear false witness," this list could describe any number of groups in polite society. However, if we consider that this group circumcises their boys on the eighth day, eats no pork or shellfish, and does not mix dairy and meat products, one would easily recognize the group as Jews. The items in this second description are variously called identity or boundary markers in the discussion of "the new perspective on Paul." It is my thesis that 4QMMT calls these markers "works of the law."

Next, in a 2001 article entitled "4QMMT, Paul, and 'Works of the Law,'" I explored the results of my conclusions on the reading of Galatians 3 and determined that being *saved* by faith is not at issue in the letter to the Galatians, but *continuing* in faith.[8] Among the ramifications of this thesis are the conclusion that Genesis 15:6 cannot possibly be the beginning of Abraham's relationship with God and thus does not have the salvific import that those following Martin Luther have long taught. Nor is Paul to be accused of reinterpreting Habakkuk 2:4 in his quotation at Galatians 3:11. His point—in parallel with the prophet—is clear: no matter what tribulations life might bring, "the righ-

---

7. Sanders, *Paul and Palestinian Judaism*, 319–20 (emphasis original).

8. M. Abegg Jr., "4QMMT, Paul, and 'Works of the Law,'" in *The Bible at Qumran: Text, Shape, and Interpretation* (ed. P. Flint; Grand Rapids: Eerdmans, 2001), 203–16.

teous man shall live/conduct himself by faith" (not by the works of the law).

I now have the opportunity to visit this topic once more and to respond to the challenges to my position that have begun appearing in print.

The first challenge comes from Jacqueline de Roo in a 2003 article entitled "'The Concept of 'Works of the Law' in Jewish and Christian Literature.'"[9] Although de Roo does not address my position directly (her focus is Dunn and a series of articles that he published on Paul and the new perspective), her conclusions stand in sharp contrast to my own. De Roo posits six questions that she believes expose the weakness of Dunn's arguments. Taken in order, these provide a useful way of working through some of the key issues of our discussion.

1. *"If 'works of the law' are 'identity badges' . . . are they Jewish national identity badges, separating Jews from Gentiles, or identity badges which separate Jews from Jews?"*[10] I answer yes. In truth, these questions direct our attention to the very nature of the issue. If we can bring the discussion into our own world, the situation would look like this: a Baptist in discussion with a Catholic concerning issues of distinction would in the main echo the theological proximity of the parties in 4QMMT. If, on the other hand, the discussion were between a Christian and a Jew, the issues would echo the theological distance between the parties in Galatians. Both would be conversations that concern issues defining the identity of the participants in the debate. It is highly unlikely that either of our proposed discussions would concern matters such as theft, murder, or honoring one's mother or father. The former discussion—between Baptist and Catholic—might take up issues such as baptism, confirmation, and congregational or apostolic authority. Whereas the latter—between Christian and Jew—would perhaps orbit about circumcision and kosher issues, the festival calendar, and messianism. All, in my understanding, could be determined by the term "works of the law." Thus the phrase is quite agile and largely concerns issues

9. J. C. R. de Roo, "The Concept of 'Works of the Law' in Jewish and Christian Literature," in *Christian-Jewish Relations through the Centuries* (ed. S. Porter and B. Pearson; Journal for the Study of the New Testament Supplement 192; Sheffield: Sheffield Academic Press, 2000), 116–47.
10. Ibid., 126.

of legal interpretation—doctrine/halakah— rather than ethics. Although de Roo clearly desires to limit Dunn to either national identity markers or practices that distinguish Jews from other Jews, I see no reason to make the parameters so confining. The comparison that I suggest demonstrates that possible conversations are simply at different points along the same line.

2. *"Is the phrase 'works of the law' found in 4Q174?"*[11] Answering the question in the affirmative, the passage in question reads: "To that end [i.e., that a temple be established that is not defiled], he has commanded that they build him a temple of man [*or* Adam], and that in it they sacrifice to him works of the law [תורה]." Alternately, some suggest that the last phrase read: "and that in it they sacrifice to him deeds of the thanksgiving [תודה]."

The question involves the difficulty in the reading of a single Hebrew letter. Is it *dalet* (ד), leading to "deeds of thanksgiving," or *resh* (ר), resulting in "works of the law"? De Roo bases her own understanding in some large part on answering the latter (the reasons for this will become evident in her fourth question). Given the problems involved in reading this rather difficult manuscript, we will likely never be certain of either reading. Torleif Elgvin, after examining the actual manuscript under high magnification, determined that the physical evidence is ambiguous.[12] He is not a stakeholder in the discussion, and so he may be trusted as an unbiased witness. The notables lined up on either side of the issue simply give credence to Elgvin's judgment: the physical evidence is ambiguous. Additionally it appears that the context is equally so. (I will return to this point as it becomes important later in the discussion.)

3. *"The connection has been made between* תורה(ה) *מעשי 'works of the law' in 4Q174 and 4QMMT and* מעשיו בתורה *in the Community Rule. What are the implications of this important connection?"*[13] De Roo states that "a close reading of the Community Rule reveals that, in this document, 'works of the law' come to focus in *ethical* issues rather than ritual matters on which the Qumranites differed with outsiders."[14] This is perhaps her most important challenge.

11. Ibid., 127.
12. Communicated in a private conversation with the author.
13. Ibid., 126, 131.
14. Ibid., 133 (emphasis added).

1QS 5.21 and 6.18, as well as the coincident Cave 4 manuscripts (4Q258 2.3 and 4Q261 frag. 1 line 3), contain the expression מעשיו בתורה ("his works vis-à-vis the law"). These passages concern both the ranking of members and the process of initiation into the covenant of the Yaḥad. The focus of 1QS 5.21 and thus the antecedent to the pronoun *his* in this instance (4Q258 2.1, 3 and 4Q261 frag. 1 line 3) is the community member: "They shall investigate his understanding and works vis-à-vis the law . . . in order to determine his rank in the community." The focus of 1QS 6.18 is the person who has passed a full year of his initiation period into the Yaḥad: "The general membership shall inquire into the details of his understanding and works of the law." If the initiate passes muster, he is initiated more fully and steps are taken to incorporate his possessions.

De Roo then reasons that it is important to read the following section (1QS 6.24–7.25) for context and that, since the focus in this section relates entirely to ethical behavior, then it follows that the term מעשי התורה or מעשיו בתורה must also. She fails, however, to account for this section being set apart visibly by *vacats* (i.e., paragraph markers) at the end of 1QS 6.23 and beginning of 6.24. The resulting new section is also literarily set off by its introductory sentence: ואלה המשפטים אשר ישפטו בם במדרש יחד על פי הדברים ("these [which follow] are the rules by which cases are to be decided at a community inquiry"). The punishments for the following admittedly ethical stipulations are clearly determined and distinctly different from those of the preceding section. The transgressions in the latter section are various periods of ban from the pure meals and reduction in food rations. The bans range from a yearlong expulsion for cursing or outburst (perhaps we are to understand this to mean using the name of God in vain) in a time of trial or for any other reason to a ten-day punishment for "anyone interrupting his companion while in session" (1QS 7.9–10).

In sharp contrast, in the previous section (1QS 6.13–23) the initiate's failure to pass muster as to his "works of the law" resulted in a loss of prospect for further initiation into the secret teaching of the Yaḥad and incorporation of property with that of the community. At CD 20.6–8 the negative repercussions for the unsuccessful initiate are detailed: "When his actions become evident, according to the interpretation of the law [מעשיו כפי

הֹתורה מדרש] which the men of holy perfection live by, no one is allowed to share either wealth or work with such a one, for all the holy ones of the Almighty have cursed him."

4. *"Are 'works of the law' actual or spiritual sacrifices, cultic or ethical deeds?"*[15] This question, as discussed above, assumes that we follow de Roo and others in determining that 4Q174 frags. 1–2 line 7 does indeed read מעשי תורה ("works of law") rather than מעשי תודה ("works of thanksgiving"). Assuming for the moment that de Roo is correct, it is not clear by context whether the works indicated are ethical or doctrinal/halakic. She would have us understand that the phrase ועשו את כול התורה ("to do all the works of the law") in the following column (4Q174 frags. 1–3 line 2) is determinative, but the context does not qualify what is meant even here. And while column 1 is mostly concerned with a commentary on the temple, column 2 is two discussions removed, having moved on to an interpretation of Psalm 2 following an intervening four-line discussion of Psalm 1. De Roo's appeal to the deeds of David (except for the murder of Uriah) being offered up (as sacrifices) at CD 5.5–6 is beside the point, as it is not made clear that "works of the law" is what was offered up there.

De Roo considers the meaning of David's deeds in Romans 4:6–8. I am not convinced by her conclusions, however, because in Romans 4 the matter at hand concerns the question of when Abraham was reckoned as righteous—before or after he was circumcised? I do agree that, given the context, the blessing of David "apart from works" is to be understood as "works of the law." But the context also makes perfectly clear that circumcision is being described as a work of the law. David appears in the middle of this discussion only to show that even he did not work in order to merit God's favor; instead his sins were forgiven because he confessed them before God (Ps. 32:5). There is no need to come to de Roo's rather surprising conclusion that because of this "'works of the law' here must be the opposite of sin."[16]

5. *"Are 'works of the law' works performed or works prescribed? In other words, are they deeds or precepts?"*[17] I suggest that this

15. Ibid., 135.
16. Ibid., 138.
17. Ibid., 126, 138.

question misses the point. The real question is whether they were ethical or halakic, not whether they were acts or simply rulings. A precept to circumcise certainly brings an act of circumcision. A precept from 4QMMT demanding that the priest involved with the preparation of the ashes of the red heifer wait until evening in order to be pure means just that. The deed must follow. A priest made unclean by preparing the red heifer could not cleanse a person until the sun set, a precept leading to an act. Similarly, in Baptist circles, the precept that baptism is by immersion brings the practice of such. The real point is that these precepts are best described as halakic or doctrinal, rather than ethical issues.

6. *"Did Jews of the Second Temple period think of 'works of the law' as meritorious?"*[18] Certainly they did, but not, however, as a means of entrance into the community or a relationship with God. This is what many Christians assume when they hear: "and it will be reckoned to you as righteousness" (4QMMT C31). This is decidedly not the case when all the evidence from antiquity is taken into account. Here Sanders and Dunn are right: neither the Qumran sectarians nor, I am convinced, Paul's Judaizers would have argued that a person was saved by keeping the law. The sectarians did, however, consider that works of the law maintained one's right standing with God both in the present and in the eschaton.

The second challenge to my thesis comes from Simon Gathercole in his new book *Where Is Boasting? Early Jewish Soteriology and Paul's Response in Romans 1–5.*[19] In chapter 2, "Works and Final Vindication in the Qumran Literature," Gathercole writes:

> The most recent affirmation of Sanders's position on the Qumran literature is M. Abegg's "4QMMT C27, 31 and 'Works Righteousness.'" Abegg will provide a convenient dialogue partner here. His article attempts to show that the category of "works-righteousness" is highly inappropriate as a description of the pattern of religion in the Qumran literature as a whole.[20]

18. Ibid., 145.
19. S. Gathercole, *Where Is Boasting? Early Jewish Soteriology and Paul's Response in Romans 1–5* (Grand Rapids: Eerdmans, 2002).
20. Ibid., 91.

He then reviews my support for this determination and challenges two points: my understanding of "works of Torah" in 4QMMT and my determination that the entry requirement for initiation into the Qumran community was repentance, not "works of the law."

As to the first, Gathercole concludes from a study of the verb עשה ("to do") in the Hebrew Bible when תורה ("law") is its object that "'works of Torah' should be understood primarily as deeds done in obedience to the *totality* of the Torah."[21] The frequency of this word pair is indeed evident—although it must be pointed out again that the specific terminology, מעשי התורה ("works of the law"), is not. Indeed, the emphasis that Gathercole reviews is quite common in the Qumran texts as well, to the point that some researchers suggest that the ancient name for the group may be reflective of this focus: they are the עושי (התורה) ('ôśê [hatôrâ], "doers [of the law]") (1QpHab 7.11; 8.1; 4Q171 2.15) or the sound-alike "Essenes."[22] It is instructive, however, to note the qualifications to this emphasis:

> "The priests": they are the repentant of Israel, who go out of the land of Judah, and the Levites are those accompanying them; "and the sons of Zadok" . . . who act according to the interpretation of the law by which the forefathers were taught, until the age is over. (CD 4.2–8)

> None who have been brought into the covenant shall enter into the sanctuary . . . if they are not careful to act according to the interpretations of the law for the era of wickedness. (CD 6.11–14)

> In the council of the Yaḥad there shall be twelve laymen and three priests who are blameless in the light of all that has been revealed from the whole law, so as to work truth, righteousness, justice, lovingkindness, and humility, one with another. (1QS 8.1–2)

The interpretation of the law, which has been revealed by God, is the focus of the phrase "works of the law." Consistently, this

21. Ibid., 92 (emphasis original).
22. On this point, see S. Goranson, "Others and Intra-Jewish Polemic as Reflected in Qumran Texts," in *The Dead Sea Scrolls after Fifty Years: A Comprehensive Assessment* (ed. P. W. Flint and J. C. VanderKam; 2 vols.; Leiden: Brill, 1998–99), 2:534–51.

combination is brought into stark contrast with the practice of the rest of the Jews, those who are called "wicked" (רשעים) and "ruthless" (עריצים) and from whom the sectarians sought to distinguish themselves:

> This [Hab. 2:4] refers to all those who obey the law among the Jews whom God will rescue from among those doomed to judgment, because of their suffering and their loyalty to the Teacher of Righteousness. (1QpHab 8.1–3)

> This [a reference to Ps. 37:12: "The wicked plots against the righteous"] refers to the cruel Israelites in the house of Judah who plot to destroy those who obey the law who are in the party of the Yaḥad. (4Q171 2.13–14)

No doubt the emphasis was on the Torah in its entirety (see 1QS 8.1–2) but "obeying the law" was *in accordance with the correct interpretation*, that which had been revealed by God. The noun phrase "works of the law" is, as Gathercole suggests, a natural development from the Hebrew Bible. But the phrase does not simply mean "works of the law as God has commanded," but rather, "works of the law that God has commanded *and revealed fully only to us*." I believe that these "works of the law" were boundary issues in the first instance. They determined the Qumran sect distinctly within Judaism as a whole, apart from the question of their salvific value. It was a particular set of "works of the law" that defined Qumran Judaism for what it was, its doctrinal stance. Though "boundary defining" in the first instance, the result was obviously seen as determining one's eschatological well-being. If you are one of us, you are going where we are going. If you are not one of us—evidenced by a different set of doctrines—you are in trouble.

Gathercole's warnings that "the polemic context in which the phrase is used in MMT . . . cannot be transferred wholesale into the Pauline context"[23] and that it should be understood "as concrete deeds done in obedience to the totality of the Law"[24] fail to convince, even in the context of Galatians and Romans, where

23. Gathercole, *Where Is Boasting?* 96.
24. Ibid., 95–96.

"works of the law" is used only in the context of circumcision, kosher issues, and proper festival observance.

Next, Gathercole posits that "the Soteriology of the Qumran literature is not so simple as Sanders and Abegg imply."[25] No doubt this is true, and a global study of the soteriology of the seven hundred scrolls is certainly beyond the parameters of this short study. Gathercole is concerned with "the need to obey Torah in order to be vindicated and rewarded on the last day"[26] and reads my studies with this foremost in his mind. Thus my comments, which focus on the function of works of the law as a test of the sectarians' "right standing" within the community, are interpreted to mean that I have missed their importance for "future eschatology." I respond that I have not missed this importance so much as I have concentrated my attention on other issues.

I counter that Gathercole may have missed the point of my own studies almost entirely: the phrase "works of the law" is not concerned with entrance but rather with maintenance issues—not "how does one get in?" but "how does one stay in?" My own studies have been concentrated nearer the beginning of the journey than the end.

As in all issues concerning the Dead Sea Scrolls, the discussion of law, works, and righteousness is only in the beginning stages. The intriguing 4QMMT is sure to keep students of ancient Judaism and Christianity meaningfully occupied for years to come.

25. Ibid., 92.
26. Ibid., 110.

5

"Spirit of Holiness" as Eschatological Principle of Obedience

Barry D. Smith

Israel's propensity to disobedience tragically led to exile from the land. In the Hebrew Bible, the promise is made that postexilic Israel will never again violate the law, because God will make disobedience an impossibility for his people. This eschatological promise is expressed in different ways.[1] The idea that God would

---

1. Deuteronomy promises that the hearts of the exiles and their descendants will be circumcised, resulting in obedience (30:6). Ezekiel prophesies that God will give them a singleness of heart (11:19), removing the heart of stone and replacing it with a heart of flesh (11:19; 36:26); he will give them a new heart (36:26). The prophet also says that God will give his people a new spirit (11:19; 36:26) and even that he will give them his own Spirit (36:27; cf. 37:14; 39:29). (In Joel 2, the giving of the Spirit does not result in spiritual transformation.) Jeremiah promises on God's behalf that at the restoration God will put his law within and write it upon the hearts of the people (31:33). Jeremiah, like Ezekiel, promises that God will give the people a singleness of heart (32:39), and he says on behalf of God: "I will put the fear of me in their hearts, in order that they not turn away from me" (32:40).

spiritually transform his people at the eschaton persists into the Second Temple period. In this period one way of expressing this idea is by God's granting to his people "a spirit of holiness." In these contexts, the phrase "spirit of holiness" denotes a new spiritual disposition imparted by God to individual Jews.[2] In other words, "spirit of holiness" is an eschatological principle of obedience.[3] The purpose of this study is to gather together and investigate such uses of "spirit of holiness" in Second Temple Jewish texts, many of which are found among the Dead Sea Scrolls.

The Book of *Jubilees*

The author of the book of *Jubilees* recognizes that something is fundamentally wrong with Israel, God's chosen people. He holds that Israel's failure to keep the covenant with God is inevitable until the dawn of eschatological salvation. In *Jubilees* 1.7–14, in dependence on Deuteronomy 31:14–21, the author describes how God reveals to Moses that the Israelites will apostatize and be exiled as punishment.[4] Upon hearing of this bleak and sordid future, Moses intercedes on behalf of the people, imploring God

2. In *4 Ezra* the idea expressed by "spirit of holiness" is expressed by "a different spirit": "And the heart of the earth's inhabitants will be changed and converted to a different spirit" (6.26; see also 7.113–14); what is being described is the eschatological transformation of Israel, the removal of the innate propensity to sin. But before the eschaton, all human beings, including Jews, are subject to what W. Harnisch calls "der Verhängnischarakter des Bösens" [the destiny character of evil] (*Verhängnis und Verheißung der Geschichte: Untersuchungen zum Zeit- und Geschichtsverständnis im 4. Esra und in der syr. Baruchapokalypse* [Forschungen zur Religion und Literatur des Alten und Neuen Testaments 97; Göttingen: Vandenhoeck & Ruprecht, 1969], 170).

3. The term "spirit of holiness" occurs infrequently in the Hebrew Bible (Isa. 63:11 [cf. 63:14]; Ps. 51:11 [51:13 Heb.]) and never with the meaning of *eschatological* principle of obedience. As already indicated, the closest parallel to the idea of the "spirit of holiness" as eschatological principle of obedience is found in Ezekiel: the prophet proclaims that God will give his people a new spirit and that he will give them his own Spirit.

4. 4Q216 preserves *Jub*. 1.7–15; in this fragment are several clear parallels to Deut. 31. Copies of the book of *Jubilees* from Cave 4 were officially published by J. C. VanderKam and J. Milik, "Jubilees," in *Qumran Cave 4.VIII: Parabiblical Texts, Part 1* (ed. H. W. Attridge et al.; Discoveries in the Judaean Desert 13; Oxford: Clarendon, 1994), 1–140. On the influence of the Deuteronomic material on *Jub*. 1, see R. A. Werline, *Penitential Prayer in Second Temple Judaism: The*

that he prevent the apostasy of the people by creating for them "an upright spirit" (*Jub*. 1.20).[5] The original Hebrew phrase was probably something like רוח ישר, which does not appear in the Hebrew Bible. Later Moses requests that God "create a pure heart and a spirit of holiness for them" (1.21), which is clearly reminiscent of Psalm 51, in which the psalmist also asks God to create for him a "pure heart" (לב טהור) and pleads with God "not to remove your spirit of holiness from me" (רוח קדשך אל־תקח ממני) (51:10–11 [51:12–13 Heb.]). Creating an upright spirit, a pure heart, and a spirit of holiness seem to be synonymous expressions each denoting a disposition to obedience, the possession of which would make disobedience impossible. Moses asks that God would give to each Israelite this new disposition to obedience, so that the possibility of national rebellion would forever vanish.

God responds by saying that, when in exile the people return to him "in all uprighteousness and with all their heart and soul," he will effect the national spiritual transformation requested by Moses: "And I shall cut off the foreskin of their heart and the foreskin of the heart of their descendants" (*Jub*. 1.23). Clearly dependent on Deuteronomy 30:1–10, the author interprets the period up to the exile as the period of Israel's inevitable failure; this is remedied only by God's act of eliminating all possibility of future apostasy by circumcising the hearts of the Israelites and their descendants (Deut. 30:6). But this national spiritual renewal is conditional upon national

---

Development of a Religious Institution (Society of Biblical Literature Early Judaism and Its Literature 13; Atlanta: Scholars Press, 1998), 110–13.

5. G. Davenport argues that *Jub*. 1.4b–26 and 23.14–20, 22–31 were additions made to what he calls "The Angelic Discourse" by the first redactor, writing sometime during the Maccabean struggles (166–160 BCE) (*The Eschatology of the Book of Jubilees* [Studia Post-Biblica 20; Leiden: Brill, 1970]). The first edition of the book of *Jubilees* was written before the Maccabean wars during the late third century or early second century BCE. The redactor sought to accomplish two purposes: (1) in the context of Seleucid oppression, to explain that the reason for national suffering was national sin; and (2) to reassure that God remained faithful to the nation and would soon bring deliverance from the Seleucids. Davenport's redactional work on the book of *Jubilees* or parts thereof may be correct, but it lacks definitive proof. This type of study is fraught with conjecture. It is probably better to treat the book of *Jubilees* as a unity, even while admitting the use of sources and stages in its evolution.

repentance. It seems that the author is reading Deuteronomy 30:1–10 in light of Leviticus 26:40–45, where it is specified that if the exiled nation confesses its iniquity and that of the fathers and turns, if their uncircumcised hearts are humble, then God will remember the covenant and bring the nation back to the land.[6] (How national repentance can occur without national spiritual transformation, however, is not explained.) The Lord continues: "And I shall create for them a spirit of holiness, and I shall purify them so that they will not turn away from following me from that day and forever" (*Jub.* 1.23; see also 50.5).[7] Parallel to the idea of an eschatological circumcision of the heart is that of the creation of a spirit of holiness and God's purification of his people. The creation of a spirit of holiness is God's implanting of a disposition toward holiness in his people; similarly, purification is the removal of the disposition to sin. The result of God's creating a spirit of holiness for the Israelites and his purification of them is that the people will henceforth keep the commandments, never again turning away from God.[8] It must be noted, however, that from the author's second-century point of view this spiritual transformation was still future, being reserved for the eschaton, in spite of the Jews having returned to the land long ago.[9]

6. E. Sjöberg writes, "Die Tat Gottes is darum eigentlich nur die Antwort auf die aufrichtige Umkehr des Volkes." [The act of God is for that reason actually only the response to the sincere repentance of the people.] *Gott und die Sünder im palästinischen Judentum* (Beiträge zur Wissenschaft vom Alten und Neuen Testament 79; Stuttgart: Kohlhammer, 1938), 255.

7. M. Testuz points out that *Jub.* 1.23 has a parallel in *Jub.* 23.26: at the end the younger generation will "search out the commandments" and "return to the way of righteousness" (see also 23.16–17); *Les idées religieuses du livre des Jubilés* (Geneva: Droz/Paris: Minard, 1960), 166–69.

8. The book of *Jubilees* has three phases of human history, defined in accordance with the basic moral and spiritual disposition of human beings: (1) in the antediluvian period, human beings could be only wicked, with the exception of Noah and his family; (2) in the postdiluvian period, human beings can obey, if they so choose; and (3) in the eschatological period, Israelites will be so transformed that disobedience will be an impossibility.

9. M. A. Knibb, "The Exile in the Literature of the Intertestamental Period," *Heythrop Journal* 17 (1976): 253–72, esp. 266–67; and B. Halpern-Amaru, "Exile and Return in Jubilees," in *Exile: Old Testament, Jewish, and Christian Conceptions* (ed. J. Scott; Journal for the Study of Judaism in the Persian, Hellenistic, and Roman Period Supplement 56; Leiden: Brill, 1997), 127–44.

Words of the Luminaries (4Q504)

The text titled *Words of the Luminaries* (דברי המארות) is a collection of prayers, one for each day of the week; each prayer is a "communal petition motivated by historical reminiscences."[10] In what remains of the two copies of this text found in Cave 4 at Qumran, there are references to the fourth day of the week (הרביעי [יו]ם) and the day of the Sabbath (הודות ביום השבת).[11] The prayer preceding the one for the Sabbath presumably is the prayer for Friday. Likely, the rest of the days of the week were assigned prayers; each day probably began with the heading "Hymns on the . . ." followed by the day of the week.[12] Paleographically, the oldest copy of *Words of the Luminaries* (4Q504) may date from as early as the middle of the second century BCE.[13] Based on the paleographical evidence and the lack of anything distinctly sectarian about the surviving texts, *Words of the Luminaries* probably antedates the formation of the Qumran community[14]—this

10. E. G. Chazon, "4QDibHam: Liturgy or Literature?" *Revue de Qumran* 15 (1991–92): 447–55, esp. 448. See also L. H. Schiffman, "The Dead Sea Scrolls and the Early History of Jewish Liturgy," in *The Synagogue in Late Antiquity* (ed. L. I. Levine; Philadelphia: American Schools of Oriental Research, 1987), 33–48, esp. 40–41.

11. Baillet originally identified 4Q505 as a third copy of *Words of the Luminaries*, but this is now contested; see the discussion in D. Falk, *Daily, Sabbath, and Festival Prayers in the Dead Sea Scrolls* (Studies on the Texts of the Desert of Judah 27; Leiden: Brill, 1998), 59–61.

12. D. T. Olson, "Words of the Lights," in *The Dead Sea Scrolls: Hebrew, Aramaic, and Greek Texts with English Translations*, vol. 4A: *Pseudepigraphic and Non-Masoretic Psalms and Prayers* (ed. J. H. Charlesworth; Louisville: Westminster/John Knox, 1997), 107–53; Emil Schürer, *The History of the Jewish People in the Age of Jesus Christ (175 B.C.–A.D. 135)* (rev. and ed. Geza Vermes et al.; 2nd ed.; Edinburgh: Clark, 1986), 3.1:459.

13. The other text, 4Q506, can be dated to the mid–first century CE; M. Baillet, *Qumrân grotte 4.III* (Discoveries in the Judaean Desert 7; Oxford: Clarendon, 1982), 168, 170.

14. See Baillet, *Qumrân grotte 4.III*, 137; M. Lehmann, "A Re-Interpretation of 4QDibrê Ham-Me'oroth," *Revue de Qumran* 5 (1964): 106–10; Olson, "Words of the Lights," 108; Falk, *Daily, Sabbath, and Festival Prayers*, 61–63. H. Lichtenberger agrees that *Words of the Luminaries* antedates the formation of the Qumran community (*Studien zum Menschenbild in Texten der Qumrangemeinde* [Studien zur Umwelt des Neuen Testaments 15; Göttingen: Vandenhoeck & Ruprecht, 1980], 93n1). He notes that the stress on Israel's election and the value of the temple (p. 4), as well as the petition for the liberation of Israel from its Gentile captivity, makes it unlikely that this collection of liturgical texts is

in spite of the two copies of the text having been written in the system of orthography and language that Emanuel Tov claims is unique to Qumran.[15] Furthermore, the lack of polemic against the idea of Israel's return from Babylon as fulfillment of the promised restoration suggests that the prayers originated in a nonsectarian context (4Q504 frags. 1–2 5.9–13).[16] It is probable that *Words of the Luminaries* was copied and used by the Qumran community.

The prayer to be recited on Friday reflects upon the exile and God's subsequent mercy to his people (4Q504 frags. 1–2 col. 5; see similar material in Ezra 9; Neh. 9; Dan. 9). This mercy culminates in the spiritual transformation of the people. After he had poured out his wrath upon the nation, God remembered his covenant and redeemed his people from among the nations where they were scattered. The influence of Leviticus 26:44–45 is evident on 4Q504 frags. 1–2 5.9b–11.[17] In the view of the author, God was merciful to the Israelites while they dwelled among the nations, in order

---

sectarian in origin. Chazon argues that one would expect to find some account of the community's history in the historical prologues to the seven prayers, especially the prayer for Friday, which concerns the postexilic period; "Is Divrei Ha-Me'orot a Sectarian Prayer?" in *The Dead Sea Scrolls: Forty Years of Research* (ed. D. Dimant and U. Rappaport; Jerusalem: Magnes, 1992), 15–16.

15. Chazon, "Is Divrei Ha-Me'orot a Sectarian Prayer?" 5–7; E. Tov, "The Scribes of the Texts Found in the Judean Desert," in *The Quest for Context and Meaning: Studies in Biblical Intertextuality in Honor of James A. Sanders* (ed. C. A. Evans and S. Talmon; Biblical Interpretation Series 28; Leiden: Brill, 1997), 131–52; idem, "Scribal Practices Reflected in the Texts from the Judaean Desert," in *The Dead Sea Scrolls after Fifty Years* (ed. P. W. Flint and J. C. VanderKam; Leiden: Brill, 1998), 1:403–29.

16. Werline, *Penitential Prayer in Second Temple Judaism*, 148.

17. The parallels between Lev. 26:45 and 4Q504 frags. 1–2 5.9b–12a are as follows:

4Q504 frags. 1–2 5.9b–12a	Leviticus 26:45
ותזכור ברית°° אשר הוצאתנו לעיני הגוים ולוא עזבתנו בגוים ותחון את עמכה ישראל בכול [ה]ארצות אשר הדחתם שמה	וזכרתי להם ברית ראשנים אשר הוצאתי־אתם מארץ מצרים לעיני הגוים להיות להם לאלהים אני יהוה
And you remembered your covenant, so that you brought us out before the eyes of the nations. And you did not leave us among the nations. And you were gracious to your people Israel in all the lands to which you exiled them.	And I will remember for them the covenant of the ancestors whom I brought out of the land of Egypt before the eyes of the nations to be God to them. I am Yahweh.

that they "might be caused to return to their heart and to return again to you and to heed your voice [according to] everything that you commanded by the hand of your servant Moses" (4Q504 frags. 1–2 5.13–14). According to this salvation-historical reflection, while Israel was still in exile, God took measures to make future disobedience impossible: "For you have poured your spirit of holiness upon us [עלינו קודשכה רוח את יצקתה כי]א[כי]], to fill us with your blessings, so that we would look for you in our anguish" (5.15–16).[18] In other words, God gave to the exiles a new disposition to obedience, in order that their chastisement would not drive them even further away from him but would, rather, lead them to repentance.[19] Thus, one could argue that repentance is the effect of the pouring out of God's spirit of holiness.[20] It seems that, unlike what is said in Leviticus 26:40–41 and more in keeping with Deuteronomy 30:1–10, God poured his spirit of holiness on the people *before* they returned to him, so that the spirit of holiness is the cause of their repentance. Because they viewed themselves as in community with the exiles, with the result that they were equal participants in whatever befell them, those who recited this prayer could use the first-person plural in describing this exilic

18. It is possible that the author of *Words of the Luminaries* was influenced by Isa. 44:3: "For I will pour out my spirit on your seed" (זרעך-על רוחי אצק).
19. A similar idea occurs in Baruch. In Bar. 2:30–35 it is said that God will make an everlasting covenant with his people at the restoration, so that he will be their God and they will be his people. In 3:5–7, however, the author says about exiled Israel, "For you put the fear of you in our hearts, in order that we would call upon your name" (ὅτι διὰ τοῦτο ἔδωκας τὸν φόβον σου ἐπὶ καρδίαν ἡμῶν τοῦ ἐπικαλεῖσθαι τὸ ὄνομά σου). This implies that the first steps toward the realization of the everlasting covenant have already been taken before the actual restoration.
20. It is interesting that the expression "which Moses wrote and your servants the prophets whom you sent, in order that evil would overtake us in the last days" occurs in the fragment of the prayer found in column 3 (4Q504 frags. 1–2 3.12–14a). The phrase "in the last days" (הימים באחרית) is used by the Hebrew prophets as a designation for the period when God would restore his exiled people to the land under ideal conditions. Although the text is fragmentary, the phrase "in the last days" probably indicates that the composer of this prayer believed that his time was the time of the eschaton. Whether the evil that overtook those who offered this prayer was the exile or some subsequent national crisis, such as the Antiochan persecution, is unknown. Regardless, there is an eschatological perspective evident in this prayer: those who prayed this prayer believed that they stood in the period of the fulfillment of the promise given through the prophets to Israel.

event. What is implied is that subsequent generations are likewise beneficiaries of this spiritual renewal, described as the pouring out of the spirit of holiness upon the people, for it continues to be in effect among postexilic generations. Whether the author of this prayer would see this promise as fulfilled of all Jews in his day or just a remnant from among them, however, is not clear.

Parallel in meaning to the idea of God's pouring out of a spirit of holiness upon the people is that of the implanting of the law in the hearts of the people found in column 2: "And to implant your law in our heart [לטעת תורתכה בלבנו], [in order that we do not stray] to the right or to the left" (4Q504 frags. 1–2 2.13–14). Clearly, this is an allusion to Jeremiah 31:31 (see also Jer. 24:4–7 and perhaps Isa. 51:7). Although, unfortunately, the text is fragmentary, it seems that this is a petition to God to turn once again in mercy to Israel and make future disobedience impossible through the internalization of the law, the implanting of the law in the collective heart of the people. That the author petitions God to do this may imply that it has not yet happened, but will in the eschatological future. If so, this stands in tension with what is affirmed in column 5, where the author speaks of God's eschatological transformation of Israel as having already occurred, even in the exile.

Qumran Sectarian Writings

The Qumran community understands its existence as owing to the eschatological mercy of God.[21] Central to these texts is the assumption that the community represents the beneficiaries of God's present and future eschatological promises. One such promise is

21. Indicators of the eschatological self-understanding of the community include (1) references to "the end of days" (אחרית הימים) or "the end time" (אחרית העת) as already present (CD 4.4; 1QpHab 2.5–6; 7.1–8; 4QMMT C14–16, 21, 30) (other such references are futuristic in orientation; CD 6.11; 4Q174 frag. 1 1.2, 11–12); (2) the interpretation of the formation of the community as the result of God's restoration, foretold in the prophets (CD 1–4); (3) references to the members of the community as having entered the covenant (1QS; CD) and, more significantly, the new covenant (CD 6.19; 8.21; 20.12; 1QpHab 2.3); and (4) the statement in 4Q174 frag. 1 col. 2 that the present is the time of the eschatological refining mentioned in Dan. 12. See A. Steudel, "אחרית הימים in the Texts from Qumran," *Revue de Qumran* 16 (1993): 225–46.

the granting of a disposition to obedience,[22] sometimes called in the Qumran sectarian texts "a spirit of holiness."[23] Significantly, in these texts this promise is understood as both already realized in the present and yet to be realized in the future.[24] Apparently, it is realized in the present in a partial way but will be realized completely in the future, at the visitation of God.

Community Rule (1QS)

The *Community Rule* is a composite document serving as something of a constitution for the Qumran community. It pro-

22. An echo of Jeremiah's prophecy that God will make a new covenant with the house of Israel and the house of Judah, which in part will result in God's placing his law within them and in writing it upon their hearts (Jer. 31:31–34), is found in 1QH[a] 12.10–12, where the founder affirms that God has engraved his law upon his heart (תורתכה אשר שננתה בלבבי). (In two places the *Damascus Document* says explicitly that those who belong to the community have actually entered the new covenant: 6.19; 8.21; cf. also 20.12.) Sjöberg refers to God's spiritual transformation of the Qumran community as "Neuschöpfung" (new creation); see "Neuschöpfung in den Toten-Meer-Rollen," *Studia theologica* 9 (1956): 131–36.

23. See A. A. Anderson, "The Use of 'Ruaḥ' in 1QS, 1QH, and 1QM," *Journal of Semitic Studies* 7 (1962): 293–303, esp. 301–2. F. F. Bruce categorizes the uses of the term "spirit of holiness" in the Dead Sea Scrolls, but fails to notice its use as the eschatological principle of obedience; "Holy Spirit in the Qumran Texts," *Annual of Leeds University Oriental Society* 6 (1969): 49–55.

24. W. Foerster explains: "Die Qumrangemeinde weiß sich also in einem eigenartigen 'Zwischen' lebend: die Heilszeit ist eingeleitet, Gott hat die Würzel der Pflanzung sprießen lassen, aber die Vollendung steht noch aus, noch ist die Zeit Belials." [The Qumran community thus understands itself to be living in a special "in-between" time: the time of salvation has been initiated, God has caused the root of planting to sprout, but the culmination still remains in the future—it is still the time of Belial.] "Der heilige Geist im Spätjudentum," *New Testament Studies* 8 (1960–61): 117–34, esp. 132. "Spirit of holiness" correspondingly is understood as both a present and a future reality. Sjöberg anachronistically interprets references to "spirit of holiness" and other similar formulations as God's Holy Spirit: "Er [Gott] hat seinen heiligen Geist auf ihn gesprengt, um ihn zu reinigen und die Schuld zu sühnen." [He (God) has poured his holy spirit upon him in order to purify him and to expiate guilt.] "Neuschöpfung in den Toten-Meer-Rollen," 135. In most of the passages in question, however, "spirit" should be taken to mean human spirit or disposition as influenced by God. M. Treves is on the right track when he insists that "spirit" in 1QS 3–4 refers to "tendencies or propensities that are implanted in every man's heart" ("The Two Spirits of the Rule of the Community," *Revue de Qumran* 3 [1961–62]: 449–52). He errs, however, in not recognizing that some uses of "spirit" refer to angelic beings.

vides not only regulations for entrance into the community and the ordering of common life, but also some of the theoretical underpinnings of this sectarian movement. The *Community Rule* contains three references to "spirit of holiness."

1QS 4.18–21

At his visitation, the time of final salvation and judgment, God will put an end to the existence of deceit (1QS 4.18–19): "God will purify by his truth all the works of man and purge for himself some from the sons of man.[25] He will utterly destroy the spirit of deceit from within his flesh" (4.20–21). What is being described is the eschatological removal of the possibility of disobedience, the spirit of deceit. The sons of truth may be generally righteous, having a greater portion of the spirit of truth, but they still have a share in the spirit of deceit. Only at the time of God's visitation will the possibility of disobedience be eliminated altogether. Annie Jaubert calls this the "renouvellement eschatologique" (eschatological renewal) of the covenant, at which time "la perversité aura été exterminée à jamais" (perversity will have been exterminated once and for all) and the time when "l'homme sera entièrement purifié et délivré pour toujours de Belial" (man will be entirely purified and forever delivered from Belial). Jaubert sees in the clause "and the making of the new" (ועשות חדשה) in 1QS 4.25 an allusion to Isaiah 43:19, in which the prophet foretells that God will do a new thing in Israel, unlike the old thing. In the community's interpretation, the new thing that God will do is the eschatological removal of the possibility of sin.[26]

The means by which God will carry out this eschatological purging is described in 1QS 4.20 as "his truth" (אמתו). This important but ambiguous term in this context seems to mean that attribute of God whereby he opposes and ultimately defeats the deceit infecting creation. Parallel to this, in 1QS 4.21 it is said that God will purify "man" (גבר)—understood generi-

---

25. Jacob Licht believes that the text should read מבנה איש ("the building of man"); "An Analysis of the Treatise on the Two Spirits in DSD," in *Aspects of the Dead Sea Scrolls* (ed. C. Rabin and Y. Yadin; Scripta hierosolymitana 4; Jerusalem: Magnes, 1965), 97.

26. A. Jaubert, *La notion d'alliance dans le judaïsme* (Patristica sorbonensia 6; Paris: Seuil, 1963), 226.

cally—from all evil acts "by means of a spirit of holiness" (רוח
קודש) and that God will also sprinkle upon "man" "a spirit of
truth" (רוח אמת) like waters of purification.[27] It seems that
these three terms—his (God's) truth, a spirit of holiness, and a
spirit of truth—are synonymous.[28] Each denotes the means by
which God will purify the members of the community at the
eschaton.[29] That is, each denotes an eschatological principle of
obedience (see 1QS 3.7–8),[30] the means by which God shall destroy at his visitation the very possibility of disobedience.[31]

1QS 2.19–3.12

Although 1QS 4.18–21 anticipates a time in the future when
God will render disobedience impossible through purifying

27. See the discussion in A. Sekki, *The Meaning of* Ruaḥ *at Qumran* (Society
of Biblical Literature Dissertation Series 110; Atlanta: Scholars Press, 1989),
207–12.

28. F. Nötscher, "Geist und Geister in den Texten von Qumran," in *Mélanges
bibliques rédigés en l'honneur de André Robert* (Paris: Bloud & Gay, 1957), 306–8;
and P. Wernberg-Møller, "A Reconsideration of the Two Spirits in the Rule of
the Community (1QSerek iii,13–iv,26)," *Revue de Qumran* 11 (1961): 413–41,
esp. 423, 440.

29. The relationship between "spirit of truth" or "spirit of holiness" as the
eschatological means of the purification of the sons of truth and the "spirit
of truth" who resides in every human being from birth is difficult to determine (1QS 3–4; see also *Testament of Judah* 20; *Testament of Asher* 1.3–9). J.
Schreiner proposes that they are the same; "Geistbegabung in der Gemeinde
von Qumran," *Biblische Zeitschrift* 9 (1965): 161–80, esp. 174–77. Similarly,
Foerster argues that "spirit of holiness" in 1QHª is synonymous with "spirit
of truth" in 1QS 3–4; "Der heilige Geist im Spätjudentum," 129–30. It is pref-
erable, however, to allow for polyvalence and even ambiguity of usage of
the terms "spirit," "spirit of holiness," "spirit of truth," or any other phrase
consisting of "spirit" in genitive construct with another noun. One should
not assume that a single consistent doctrine of "spirit" underlies each of the
occurrences of "spirit" used by itself or in construct form. The spirit of truth
present in each human being from birth is not the spirit of truth by which
God will purify eschatologically.

30. A. R. C. Leaney, *The Rule of Qumran and Its Meaning* (London: SCM,
1966), 158–59, feels obliged to connect the use of "spirit of holiness" in 1QS 4.21
with other uses of "spirit of holiness," "spirit," and other phrases with "spirit"
in them, on the assumption that there is a shared root meaning. This is a difficult task and probably in the end results in misinterpretation, since there is
no root meaning.

31. Strangely, in his "Treatise on the Two Spirits in DSD," Licht does not
comment on the use of the phrase "spirit of holiness" in 1QS 4.21.

human beings by "a spirit of holiness," in 1QS 3.6–8 it is said that a spirit of holiness is already present in the community, effecting repentance and atonement. This is a present manifestation of the eschatological mercy of God. 1QS 2.19–3.12 specifies what appears to be the procedure for the annual renewal of the covenant by the community in which all members of the community must participate.[32] The members renew their original commitment to enter the covenant in order to obey the law perfectly. In this context, the one who refuses to enter the covenant is discussed. This one is said to be "unable to repent, in order that he might live" (לוא חזק למשוב חיו) (3.1).[33] The same

32. Jaubert, *La notion d'alliance dans le judaïsme*, 211–27. Jaubert argues convincingly that the Qumran sectarians saw themselves as being in the covenant, which they annually renewed during a ceremony on the Day of Pentecost, the fifteenth day of the third month (see also *Jub.* 6.17–20; 44.1–8). She explains that, in their understanding, the one covenant had more than one historical phase, and the phase into which they entered upon their repentance was second only in importance to the initial phase of the covenant, its establishment with Abraham. This was because their covenant was the new covenant, the fulfillment of the promise of eschatological spiritual renewal of the nation. It is this eschatological phase of the covenant that the sectarians renewed once a year. Participation in the covenant-renewal ceremony was equally a commitment to obey the law as interpreted by the community. In addition to 1QS 2.19–25a, see also 4Q267 frag. 18 5.17–18; 4Q270 frag. 11 2.11–12; and 1Q34 frag. 3 2.3–7 for other references to the annual covenant renewal. See also B. Nitzan, "4QBerakot[a–e] (4Q286–290): A Covenant Ceremony in the Light of Related Texts," *Revue de Qumran* 16 (1995): 487–506; idem, "The Concept of the Covenant in Qumran Literature," in *Historical Perspectives from the Hasmoneans to Bar Kokhba in Light of the Dead Sea Scrolls* (ed. D. Goodblatt, A. Pinnick, and D. Schwartz; Studies on the Texts of the Desert of Judah 37; Leiden: Brill, 2001), 85–104; W. Eiss, "Das Wochenfest im Jubiläenbuch und im antiken Judentum," in *Studies in the Book of Jubilees* (ed. M. Albani, J. Frey, and A. Lange; Texte und Studien zum antiken Judentum 65; Tübingen: Mohr-Siebeck, 1997), 164–78; Falk, *Daily, Sabbath, and Festival Prayers*, 219–36; S. Pfann, "The Essene Yearly Renewal Ceremony and the Baptism of Repentance," in *The Provo International Conference on the Dead Sea Scrolls* (ed. D. Parry and E. Ulrich; Studies on the Texts of the Desert of Judah 30; Leiden: Brill, 1999), 337–52; and J. C. VanderKam, "Covenant and Biblical Interpretation in Jubilees 6," in *The Dead Sea Scrolls Fifty Years after Their Discovery* (ed. L. H. Schiffman, E. Tov, and J. C. VanderKam; Jerusalem: Israel Exploration Society, 2000), 92–104.

33. "He is unable to repent, in order that he might live"—adopted by P. Wernberg-Møller and J. H. Charlesworth—is not the only translation possible for the clause לוא חזק למשוב חיו. It may be rendered "he has not persisted in the conversion of his life" (Vermes); "he has not devoted himself to the conversion of his life" (Knibb); and "he has not mastered his backslidings" (Leaney). Wern-

"cannot be purified by atonement" (לוא יזכה בכפורים) (3.4).
Repentance is conditional upon entrance into the community,
which explains why the one who refuses to enter is said to be
unable to repent; repentance then brings atonement.[34]

How entering the community, the ability to repent, and obtaining atonement relate to one another is further explained. The
reason that atonement is denied to the one who refuses to enter
the covenant is given as follows: "It is by a spirit of holiness of the
community in his [God's] truth that he is cleansed from all his
iniquities. It is by an upright and humble spirit that his sin can be
atoned" (וברוח קדושה ליחד באמתו יטהר מכול עוונותו וברוח יושר
ועמה תכופר חטתו) (1QS 3.7–8). Atonement occurs by means of
"a spirit of holiness" (רוח קדושה) (3.7), which is synonymous
with "an upright and humble spirit" (רוח יושר ועמה) (3.8). The
meaning seems to be that atonement occurs when a person enters
the community and comes under the influence of a principle of
obedience, which naturally leads to repentance, the turning from
sin toward obedience to the law.[35] In response to this repentance,
God atones for sin.[36] The idea that God responds to repentance

berg-Møller, however, offers convincing arguments for his translation, finding
a parallel to it in *4 Ezra* 7.81–82; *The Manual of Discipline* (Studies on the Texts
of the Desert of Judah 1; Leiden: Brill, 1957), 58.

34. For a discussion of 1QS 3.4–12, see G. Klinzing, *Die Umdeutung des
Kultus in der Qumrangemeinde und im Neuen Testament* (Studien zur Umwelt
des Neuen Testaments 7; Göttingen: Vandenhoeck & Ruprecht, 1971), 99–102.

35. R. Kvalvaag concludes concerning the meaning of 1QS 3.7–8: "The spirit
of holiness cleansing the devout person of all his sins is no doubt the Holy
Spirit"; "The Spirit in Human Beings in Some Qumran Non-Biblical Texts," in
Qumran between the Old and New Testaments (ed. F. Cryer and T. Thompson;
Journal for the Study of the Old Testament Supplement 290; Sheffield: Sheffield
Academic Press, 1998), 159–80, esp. 171. If he means by "Holy Spirit" what the
early church meant, then it seems that he is wrong. The context suggests that
all the phrases containing "spirit" (רוח) in 1QS 3.6–8 are synonymous: "spirit of
the true counsel of God," "spirit of holiness," and "upright and humble spirit."
Kvalvaag also misleadingly interprets some instances of the phrase "spirit of
holiness" in the *Hodayot* as referring to the Holy Spirit (173–79). See Schreiner,
"Geistbegabung in der Gemeinde von Qumran."

36. The connection between a spirit of holiness and atonement is missed
when the former is not understood as a principle of obedience. See, for example,
O. Betz, who affirms that the spirit serves as a "Reinigungsmittel" (means of
purification) but without explaining why; *Offenbarung und Schriftforschung in
der Qumransekte* (Wissenschaftliche Untersuchungen zum Neuen Testament 6;
Tübingen: Mohr-Siebeck, 1960), 131. See also Bruce, "Holy Spirit in the Qum-

by atoning for past sin is not unusual in Second Temple Jewish understanding. The unique aspect of the Qumran sectarian perspective is the idea that there is a principle of obedience at work in the community effecting repentance, being a manifestation of the eschatological mercy of God. Since it is called "a spirit of holiness *of the community*" (רוח קדושה ליחד), this principle of obedience is accessible only to those who enter the community.[37] The phrase "in his truth" attached to "by a spirit of holiness of the community" should probably be taken to mean that the cause of the existence of this spirit of holiness is God's "truth," meaning in this context his eschatological mercy.

The variant reading in 4QSᵃ (= 4Q255) frag. 2 line 1—"by his holy spirit" (ברוח קודשו) rather than "by a holy spirit" (ברוח קדושה)—probably indicates that, in the community's view, this new disposition to obedience, which is characteristic of those who have entered the covenant, originates with God. That is, the principle of obedience comes to human beings from without, being a gift of God's mercy.

This "spirit of holiness," or "upright and humble spirit," is also synonymous with "a spirit of the true counsel of God" (רוח עצת אמת אל) (1QS 3.6), which is likewise said to atone for iniquity: "For by the spirit of the true counsel of God are the ways of man—all his iniquity—atoned [דרכי איש יכופרו כול עוונותו]" (3.6–7). On the assumption that עצת אמת should be translated as "true counsel," perhaps the designation "a spirit of the true

---

ran Texts," 53; and H. Braun, *Spätjüdisch-häretischer und frühchristlicher Radikalismus* (Beiträge zur historischen Theologie 24.1; Tübingen: Mohr-Siebeck, 1957), 41–47. Klinzing says that both a blameless life or obedience and a spirit of holiness were means of expiation in the community, but does not seem to notice that this is really one means of atonement: repentance; *Die Umdeutung des Kultus*, 93–106. Likewise, P. von der Osten-Sacken does not make explicit that a "spirit of holiness" cleanses those who enter the community because it leads to repentance and God mercifully allows repentance to have an expiatory effect; *Gott und Belial: Traditions-geschichtliche Untersuchungen zum Dualismus in den Texten aus Qumran* (Studien zur Umwelt des Neuen Testaments 6; Göttingen: Vandenhoeck & Ruprecht, 1969), 134–35. Finally, Sekki does not view the phrase "spirit of holiness" as a principle of obedience, the impartation of a new *human* spirit or disposition, but, in most cases, views it as God's Spirit; *Meaning of Ruaḥ at Qumran*, 71–93. It seems that the Christian teaching of the Holy Spirit influenced his interpretation of pre-Christian Jewish texts.

37. P. Garnet, *Salvation and Atonement in the Qumran Scrolls* (Wissenschaftliche Untersuchungen zum Neuen Testament 2.3; Tübingen: Mohr-Siebeck, 1977), 58.

counsel of God" emphasizes the cognitive dimension of this new spiritual disposition. The spirit consists of the true counsel of God, for without an understanding of God's will there can be no proper repentance, since a person must know what God requires in order to repent. To have this new disposition to obedience results in being able "to look upon the light of life" (3.7). To look upon the light is to understand God's will, the doing of which leads to life: the light is for the purpose of life. But the phrase רוח עצת אמת אל could be translated as "the spirit of God's true council," meaning the spirit possessed by or characterizing God's true council or community. If so, it is parallel to the phrase "the spirit of holiness of the community" (3.7b).[38]

1QS 9.3–4

In 1QS 9.3–4, it is said that, when established, the community will be "a foundation of a spirit of holiness in [or of] eternal truth" (ליסוד רוח קודש לאמת עולם). The term "spirit of holiness" seems to refer to the principle of obedience that God has granted to the community by means of which atonement ultimately is procured, since atonement is conditional upon repentance and repentance on coming under the influence of this principle of obedience. Thus, the community can be described as "a foundation of a spirit of holiness," insofar as this spirit of holiness given by God is responsible for the existence of the community: it is a foundation consisting of a spirit of holiness. Without it, there would be no repentance, no possibility for the members of "cleansing their way by separating themselves from deceit" (9.9). The phrase "in [or of] eternal truth" modifying "a foundation of a spirit of holiness" makes it unambiguous that this foundation has as its basis God's eschatological mercy, expressed by means of the term "truth."[39]

Summary

In these passages from the *Community Rule*, the term "spirit of holiness" denotes an eschatological principle of obedience; it is

38. Wernberg-Møller, *Manual of Discipline*, 61–62.
39. Klinzing (*Die Umdeutung des Kultus*, 65) sees a connection between the spirit of holiness and temple imagery applied to the community, nonsacrificial atonement, and the obedience of the community, but he does not explain the nature of this connection.

the disposition to obedience that God in his mercy has bestowed upon the community. There is, however, a present and a future dimension to this eschatological gift. On the one hand, a spirit of holiness is the means by which God will purify human beings at his visitation (1QS 4.18–21). On the other hand, a spirit of holiness is assumed already to be present in the community (1QS 3.6–8; 9.3).[40] One need not, however, resort to the positing of different sources and careless redaction to account for this apparent discrepancy. Rather, to use a well-worn phrase, this juxtaposition of the eschatological present and future betrays the "already, but not yet" perspective so characteristic of this community. It is a distinctive of the Qumran community's self-understanding that its membership represents the recipients of God's eschatological mercy, foretold in the Hebrew Bible. Not with all Israel, but with only a minority within the nation did God renew his covenant, or establish the new covenant, foretold by the prophet Jeremiah. (Of course, potentially, all Jews could be the beneficiaries of God's eschatological blessings on the condition of joining the community.) Yet the establishment of the community is merely the first phase of the realization of God's salvation. (In fact, the members of the community are to be soldiers in the final, but protracted, war.) A spirit of holiness is given to the community in the present in order to make repentance and atonement possible, and this same spirit

40. CD 5.11b–19 refers to those who heard the community's interpretation of the Torah, but rejected it: "Also they have made their spirit of holiness unclean [וגם את רוח קדשיהם טמאו], and with blaspheming tongue they have opened their mouths against the statutes of the covenant of God, saying, 'They are not unfounded'" (5.11b–12). The term "spirit of holiness" as used in this context seems to intend something like an original disposition to good or the conscience. Rejecting the "statutes of the covenant" results in the defilement of this spirit of holiness, damage to this original disposition to good, or an impairment of the function of the conscience. Likewise, in CD 6.11b–8.2a, each member of the community is warned not to "defile his spirit of holiness" (את איש ישקץ ולא רוח קדשיו) (7.3b–4a). From the context it is clear that defiling one's spirit of holiness results from violating the laws of purity, especially dietary laws (7.3). To defile one's spirit of holiness through ritual impurity is to defile that original disposition to good or perhaps a restored disposition to good. The phrase "to defile one's spirit of holiness" seems to be an interpretation of Lev. 11:43 and 20:25, in which the verb "to defile" (שקץ) is used in the context of ritual defilement; in these passages, however, the object of the defilement is not "spirit of holiness," but "soul" (נפש). See Betz, Offenbarung und Schriftforschung in der Qumransekte, 126–30.

of holiness will be the means by which God destroys forever the possibility of disobedience in the future.[41] Paradoxically, it seems that until God's visitation the possibility of sin remains open to the members of the community, even though they have come under the influence of this spirit of holiness (see 1QS 3.21–23).

Blessings (1QSb)

The sectarian text known as the *Blessings* (1QSb), serving as something of an appendix to the *Community Rule*, contains blessings that are to be recited after the visitation of God, when the sons of darkness and evil will have been removed from the world; for this reason, these are *eschatological* blessings. At that time, the *maśkîl* is to bless "[those] who fear [God, do] his will, and keep his ordinances and hold fast to his s[pirit] of holiness [קודשו] [ברוח] [ומחזקי] and walk perfectly" (1.1–2).[42] The blessing, in other words, will be directed toward those who obey God, the members of the community. What is significant is that the members of the community after God's visitation are referred to as those strengthened by God's spirit of holiness. From the context, God's spirit of holiness seems to be an eschatological principle of obedience. That is, at the visitation of God the members will be able to obey God, because they will have been strengthened by God's "spirit of holiness."[43]

Thanksgiving Hymns (1QH^a)

The *Thanksgiving Hymns* contain several references to "spirit of holiness" as a present reality in the life of the community.[44] In

41. Osten-Sacken, *Gott und Belial*, 178–79.
42. Some reconstruct the text as [בבן]ריה קֹ[דֶ]שו; see J. T. Milik, "Recueil des Bénédictions (1QSb)," in *Qumran Cave 1* (ed. D. Barthélemy and J. T. Milik; Discoveries in the Judaean Desert 1; Oxford: Clarendon, 1955); and E. Lohse, *Die Texte aus Qumran* (Munich: Kösel, 1964).
43. In 1QSb 2.24, another reference to a spirit of holiness occurs: "May he be gracious to you through the spirit of holiness." Unfortunately, the context to which this statement belongs is lost, so that the full meaning of this text is unrecoverable.
44. On this topic, see M. Mansoor, *The Thanksgiving Hymns* (Studies on the Texts of the Desert of Judah 3; Grand Rapids: Eerdmans, 1961), 74–77.

some of these, it is clear that the spirit of holiness is a principle of obedience. A spirit of holiness is granted to the founder and the members of his community, with the result that obedience becomes possible. Without this provision of mercy, obedience would be impossible, since human beings are thought to be naturally weak and sinful.[45] Since the community understands its origin and nature in eschatological terms, God's granting a spirit of holiness in the *Thanksgiving Hymns* should be interpreted as the fulfillment of his eschatological promise to make any future disobedience impossible. Of course, the community applies this promise to its own members, not to the whole nation.

1QH[a] 8

In 1QH[a] 8.15, the author refers to being "strengthened by a [*or* your] spirit of holiness" ([ ]ק ברוח ולהתחזק).[46] Following this, there occur three more infinitives construct: "To adhere to the truth of your covenant, to serve you in truth with a perfect heart, to love your [ ]."[47] Unfortunately, the text is full of lacunae, so that it is not clear how these three infinitives construct relate to the previous infinitive construct: "to be strengthened by a spirit of holiness."[48] It is probable, however, that being strengthened

45. This is a long-recognized aspect of Qumran anthropology and serves as a presupposition of the teaching on the spirit of holiness in the Dead Sea Scrolls; see A. Dietzel, "Beten im Geist," *Theologische Zeitschrift* 13 (1957): 12–32, esp. 12–14; Sjöberg, "Neuschöpfung in den Toten-Meer-Rollen"; and Betz, *Offenbarung und Schriftforschung in der Qumransekte*, 120–23.

46. Geza Vermes translates as "cleaving to Thy Spirit of [holiness]," but this seems to obscure the intended meaning; *The Complete Dead Sea Scrolls in English* (4th ed.; Middlesex, UK: Penguin, 1997), 251.

47. J. Becker, *Das Heil Gottes* (Studien zur Umwelt des Neuen Testaments 3; Göttingen: Vandenhoeck & Ruprecht, 1964), 162. Becker correctly interprets the reference to a spirit of holiness in 1QH[a] 8.15 as "Kraft . . . die sowohl negativ reinigend, als auch positiv den Wandel festigend, dem Frommen helfend beisteht" (162). [Power . . . which brings help to the righteous, negatively purifying as much as positively establishing the way.] This coheres with his hypothesis that the community constituted a sort of *Heilssphäre*. Becker does not connect this spirit with repentance and does not connect repentance with the removal of guilt. He considers this spirit as a power (*Kraft*) that removes sin; it is synonymous with the *Heilssphäre*. As already indicated, Becker's analysis may be a case of overinterpretation.

48. As Becker explains, in some contexts "(God's) truth" is the equivalent of God's commandments or God's will as expressed concretely in the law; *Das*

by a spirit of holiness is to be enabled to obey the law, which the three infinitives construct express in different ways (this is the central theme of this passage).[49] (In 1QH[a] 9.31–32, God is said to strengthen the spirit of humans, but with no reference to the means, the spirit of holiness.) Elsewhere the author adds, "I know that no one is righteous except through you" (כי ואדעה בלעדיך איש יצדק לא) (8.19). On this assumption, he implores God by means of the spirit that God has given him (אשר ברוח נתתה בי]) "to perfect your [loving]kindnesses to your servant [forever], to purify me by your spirit of holiness [ברוח למהרני קודשך], and to draw me near to yourself by your grace according to your lovingkindnesses" (8.19–20). The spirit that God has given the author is doubtless to be identified with God's spirit of holiness. What is significant is that God's spirit of holiness is said to be the means of purification.[50] The meaning is probably that receiving a spirit of holiness issues in repentance, which results in being purified from sins, since repentance is the condition of the removal of guilt resulting from sin.[51]

1QH[a] 15.6–7

A similar use of the term "spirit of holiness" occurs in 1QH[a] 15.6–7. The author begins his hymn on a note of thankfulness: "I thank you, O Lord, that you have supported me with your strength, that you have spread your spirit of holiness upon me in order that I might not stumble."[52] God enables the founder to

---

Heil Gottes, 155–60. With respect to 1QH[a] 8.15, he writes: "Da der Mensch wohl kaum an Gottes Treue zu seinem Bund kleben soll, wird man אמת hier als Inhalt des Bundes fassen müssen, d.h. אמת ist hier die in den Gesetzen konkret gewordene Wahrheit Gottes" (159). [Because man is hardly obliged to cling to God's truthfulness to his covenant, one must here conceive of אמת as the content of the covenant, i.e., אמת is here the truth of God made concrete in the commandments.]

49. See Dietzel, "Beten im Geist," 23–24.

50. In 1QH[a] 17.32 the author says that God has delighted him with "your spirit of holiness" (קודשכה ברוח). Why he was delighted is not disclosed, but presumably it was because this spirit of holiness is a principle of obedience.

51. See Dietzel, "Beten im Geist," 18.

52. In 1QH[a] 4.26 an author other than the founder of the community writes, "[I thank you, Lord, that] you have shed [הניפותה] [your] spirit of holiness [[קודשכה רוח]] upon your servant." As in 1QH[a] 15.7, the verb הניף ("to shed" or "to spread upon") is used to describe the giving of a spirit of holiness, presum-

carry out his appointed task of leadership within the community against all opposition by means of his spirit of holiness.[53] To stumble would be not only to fail but also to sin against God. This spirit of holiness is a principle of obedience, a new spiritual disposition. This interpretation is confirmed by what the founder says in 1QH[a] 12.31–32: "And the path of man is not secure except by the spirit that God creates for him, to perfect the path of the sons of man, in order that all his creatures know the strength of his power." In this passage, "the spirit that God creates" is the capacity for obedience implanted in a human being by God and is doubtless a synonym for the phrase "spirit of holiness." (By it a person's way is made perfect.) In other words, human beings cannot obey God unless God first imparts to them a principle of obedience.[54] In this way, it becomes known to all that God is active in enabling obedience, which is called "the strength of his power."[55]

Summary

That God makes obedience possible for the leader of the community and the members of the community is sometimes ex-

---

ably with the same meaning. The probable use of the pronominal suffix denotes that the new spiritual disposition has its origin with God and is not an innate human capacity. Probably, the shedding of this spirit occurred at the time of the author's entrance into the community.

53. The somewhat oblique reference in 1QH[a] 6.11 to the existence of two spirits corresponding to good and evil (כי לפי רוחות [יבד]ילם בין טוב לרשע) ["Because, corresponding to the spirits, you allot to them good and evil"]) could imply that there is a counterpart to this spirit of holiness operative among human beings, similar to the spirit of deceit in 1QS 3–4. The fragmentary nature of the text makes it difficult to determine exactly the intended meaning, but it seems to be alluding to two forces or influences responsible for all human volitional activity. That the author immediately refers to God's spirit of holiness could be taken as confirmation of this interpretation (6.13). Another possible reference to the negative counterpart to a spirit of holiness could be יצר אשמה, translatable as "guilty inclination": "There is no salvation for guilty inclination; it will be trampled to destruction" (ואין פלט ליצר אשמה לכלה ירמוסו) (14.32; see also 15.16). The guilty inclination seems to be the natural disposition to evil in human beings, which will bring God's judgment. When this disposition is supplanted by God's spirit of holiness, the result is obedience and salvation.

54. M. Delcor, *Les hymnes de Qumran (Hodayot)* (Paris: Letouzey & Ané, 1962), 148.

55. Garnet, *Salvation and Atonement in the Qumran Scrolls*, 24–27.

pressed in the *Thanksgiving Hymns* as God's giving them a spirit of holiness. This spirit of holiness is an eschatological principle of obedience, the fulfillment of God's promise to transform his people spiritually at the eschaton.

Barkhi Nafshi (Bless, O My Soul) (4Q434–38)

Five collections of fragments of a work given the name *Barkhi Nafshi* (*Bless, O My Soul*) (4Q434–38) were discovered in Cave 4 at Qumran.[56] This name was chosen because the opening line of 4Q434, which probably represents the beginning of the text, begins "Bless, O my soul, the Lord" (ברכי נפשי את אדוני). The author was probably imitating Psalms 103 and 104, which also begin in this manner, but use the tetragrammaton rather than "my Lord" (אדוני). Each of the five collections is from a different scribal hand, but each also contains text that is parallel to text in at least one other copy, indicating that each collection of fragments is of the same document:[57]

4Q434 contains text found in 4Q435 and 4Q437

4Q435 has textual parallels to 4Q436 and 4Q437

4Q436 contains text also found in 4Q435

4Q437 has parallels to 4Q434, 4Q435, and 4Q438

4Q438 has text in common with 4Q437

It is probable that each of the five collections represents only a small portion of a much larger document, which may explain why what remains of it has such little literary unity. *Barkhi Nafshi* is probably sectarian.[58]

56. M. Weinfeld and D. Seely, "Barkhi Nafshi," in *Qumran Cave 4.XX: Poetic and Liturgical Texts, Part 2* (ed. E. G. Chazon et al.; Discoveries in the Judaean Desert 29; Oxford: Clarendon, 1999), 255–334.

57. D. Seely, "4Q437: A First Look at an Unpublished *Barki Nafshi* Text," in *The Provo International Conference on the Dead Sea Scrolls* (ed. D. Parry and E. Ulrich; Studies on the Texts of the Desert of Judah 30; Leiden: Brill, 1999), 146–60, esp. 148–49.

58. D. Seely, "The *Barki Nafshi* Texts (4Q434–439)," in *Current Research and Technological Developments on the Dead Sea Scrolls* (ed. D. Parry and S. Ricks; Studies on the Texts of the Desert of Judah 20; Leiden: Brill, 1996), 194–214, esp. 211–13. This is contrary to G. Brooke's assessment of the evidence; "Body

What remains of *Barkhi Nafshi* gives expression to the idea of God as merciful to his people. 4Q434 frag. 1 col. 1 (= 4Q435 frag. 1; 4Q437 frag. 1) represents the beginning of the text. On the assumption of the sectarian origin of the text, this opening section appears to be a description of the beginnings of the community, similar to what is found in CD 1.1–2.1, although there are no significant verbal parallels between the two accounts.[59] The description in *Barkhi Nafshi* is more general, more poetic, and less historical than that in the *Damascus Document*. Of significance is the author's explanation that God's mercy was manifested to the pristine members of the community as his spiritual transformation of them: "He circumcised the foreskins of their hearts" (וימול עורלות לבם) (4Q434 frag. 1 1.4). This passage is obviously dependent on Deuteronomy 30:6, which promises that God will circumcise the hearts of postexilic Israel (see also *Jub.* 1.23).[60] It is also said that God "has established their feet on the path" (ויכן לדרך רגלם) (4Q434 frag. 1 1.4), which is an idiom meaning that God has so transformed them spiritually that they now live obediently (see Ps. 85:13 [85:14 Heb.]; 1QH[a] 12.31–32).[61] Finally, God "made darkness light before them" (ויתן לפניהם מחשכים לאור) (4Q434 frag. 1 1.9). This is probably an allusion to Isaiah 42:16, which describes the eschatological transformation of Israel; the community is applying this prophecy to itself.

In a section of *Barkhi Nafshi* preserved in 4Q435 frag. 1 col. 1 and 4Q436 frag. 1 cols. 1–2, this spiritual transformation is further described probably using the phrase "spirit of holiness." The author says, "[. . .] you have driven with rebukes from me,

---

Parts in *Barkhi Nafshi* and the Qualifications for Membership of the Worshipping Community," in *Sapiential, Liturgical, and Poetical Texts from Qumran* (ed. D. Falk, F. García Martínez, and E. Schuller; Studies on the Texts of the Desert of Judah 35; Leiden: Brill, 2000), 79–94, esp. 79.

59. A perhaps accidental parallel is the use of the verb כלה: "He did not give them up to destruction [לכלה]" (CD 1.5); and "and he did not destroy them [כלם]" (4Q434 frag. 1 1.5).

60. The idea of the circumcision of the heart also occurs in Deut. 10:16; Jer. 4:4; 1QS 5.5; 1QpHab 11.13; and 4Q504 frag. 4 line 11.

61. On the theme of God's spiritual transformation of the community in *Barkhi Nafshi*, see D. Seely, "Implanting Pious Qualities as a Theme in the *Barki Nafshi* Hymns," in *The Dead Sea Scrolls Fifty Years after Their Discovery* (ed. L. H. Schiffman, E. Tov, and J. C. VanderKam; Jerusalem: Israel Exploration Society, 2000), 322–31.

and put a pure heart [לב טהור] in its place" (4Q436 frag. 1 1.10
= 4Q435 frag. 1 1.1), which is dependent on Psalm 51:10 (51:12
Heb.), where "pure heart" stands parallel to "steadfast spirit."[62]
Who is speaking in this passage and whether the "I" is gnomic is
unclear. The author continues: "And the evil inclination [יצר רע]
you have driven with rebukes from within me and a spirit of holiness you have set within my heart [ורוח קוד[ש שמחה בל בבי]"
(4Q436 frag. 1 1.10–2.1 = 4Q435 frag. 1 1.2). The phrase "spirit of
holiness" is reconstructed from Psalm 51:11 (51:13 Heb.), which
seems justified, since the author is dependent on Psalm 51 for
his phraseology.[63] In this context, the phrase "spirit of holiness"
denotes an eschatological principle of obedience, being parallel to
"pure heart." Synonymous with driving the evil inclination from
a person by rebuke is God's act of destroying the spirit of deceit:
"A spirit of deceit you have destroyed" (רוח שקר אבדת) (4Q435
frag. 1 1.5). "Spirit of deceit" is used as a technical term in 1QS
3–4 for the innate disposition to evil in human beings. According
to this passage, God has destroyed that disposition to evil in the
author or in the members of the community.[64]

Conclusion

In the passages examined, the term "spirit of holiness" denotes
an eschatological principle of obedience. Expressed differently,
it is a divinely granted capacity of repentance, which in some

62. Weinfeld and Seely propose "heart of stone" as the object of the verb "to
drive with rebukes" (גער), based on parallels to Ezek. 11:19; 36:26; 1QHᵃ 21.11;
"Barkhi Nafshi," 302.
63. Ibid., 303.
64. Another description of the spiritual transformation effected by God on
either an individual in the community or all the members of the community
occurs in 4Q437 frag. 4 = 4Q438 frag. 12 line 2. God's transforming action is
described as prospering him by means of a "firm disposition" (יצר סמוך) (see
Isa. 26:3; 1QS 4.5; 8.3; 1QHᵃ 9.35; 10.9, 36). The correlative to being granted
a firm disposition is the removal of evil (רע) (4Q437 frag. 4 line 3). Similarly,
the author says that God has removed from him "the spirit of destruction" (רוח
מחית) and clothed him with "the spirit of salvation" (רוח ישועות) (4Q437 frag.
4 lines 5–6) (see Zech. 3:4 for the use of the metaphor of being clothed). The
spirit of destruction seems to be another way to denote the innate disposition
to disobedience, whereas the spirit of salvation is its opposite, synonymous with
"firm disposition" or "spirit of holiness."

cases is said to result in atonement.[65] In some of the texts, the granting of a spirit of holiness is viewed as yet to take place, in the eschatological future, whereas in other texts, it is a present reality, an incipient manifestation of eschatological mercy. Defined as such, the term "spirit of holiness" is synonymous with the various expressions in the Hebrew Bible that describe the means by which Israel will be spiritually transformed at the eschaton. Clearly not every use of the term "spirit of holiness" in Second Temple Jewish texts has this meaning.[66] Never-

65. Leaney errs in objectifying the "spirit of holiness" in the Dead Sea Scrolls, so that it refers to an entity that exists apart from its effects; in other words, he does not interpret the term functionally. Leaney writes, for example: "The holiness of God's spirit is emphasized again and again: only God's spirit is holy and only he can bestow it upon a man" (*Rule of Qumran and Its Meaning*, 35). This is probably the result of the influence of the Christian conception of the Holy Spirit on his interpretation of these uses of the term "spirit of holiness." Betz also errs and does not see the functionality of the term; rather he objectifies the spirit of holiness, interpreting it as a substance or an entity that originates from above and overcomes the flesh and its inherent weakness and impurity: "Der Geist dagegen kommt von oben, denn er ist Gottes Geist und, wie aus seiner Bezeichung hervorgeht, heilig wie der heilige Gott." [The spirit, by contrast, is from above, because it is God's Spirit, and, as its designation implies, is holy as the holy God.] *Offenbarung und Schriftforschung in der Qumransekte*, 125. G. Maier likewise wrongly concludes that the spirit of holiness is "also nicht der schlechthin menschliche. . . . Der 'Heilige Geist' ist wirklich Gottes Geist, geht aber gewissermaßen in das Inventar des Frommen über." [thus, not simply human. . . . The "holy spirit" is actually God's Spirit but goes over in the inventory of the righteous.] *Mensch und freier Wille* (Wissenschaftliche Untersuchungen zum Neuen Testament 12; Tübingen: Mohr-Siebeck, 1971), 188–89. At least with respect to the instances studied in this essay, it is better to say that the term "spirit of holiness" is a means of describing God's action on individual Jews, creating in them a disposition to obedience. In other words, it is a divinely granted attitude or spirit that leads to obedience to the law or holiness.

66. There are other meanings for the term "spirit of holiness." First, in the Dead Sea Scrolls, the phrase "the spirit of holiness" is used to denote the means of prophetic inspiration: "According to that which the prophets have revealed by his spirit of holiness [ברוח קודשו]" (1QS 8.16). In CD 2.12 a similar meaning is probably intended: "And he informed them through those anointed of the spirit of holiness" (ויודיעם ביד משיחו רוח קדשו). This text is ambiguous for two reasons: (a) there is no preposition with "holy spirit," so that it can be the object of the verb (see Vermes's translation); and (b) it is necessary to emend משיחו ("his anointed") to משיחי ("anointed of"); see M. A. Knibb, *The Qumran Community* (Cambridge Commentaries on Writings of the Jewish and Christian World 2; Cambridge: Cambridge University Press,

theless, this is a distinctive use of the term and ought to serve as a religious-historical point of departure for understanding some of the occurrences of the term "Holy Spirit" in the New Testament.[67]

1987), 27. The context suggests that the prophets (and not God's messiah) are meant, to whom will be granted "the power to make the spirit of his holiness known to the 'remnant.'" Second, the spirit of holiness denotes the means of obtaining spiritual knowledge otherwise inaccessible to human beings (see 1QH^a 20.11–12; 5.18; 6.12–13); the same idea is found in Wis. 9:17: βουλὴν δέ σου τίς ἔγνω εἰ μὴ σὺ ἔδωκας σοφίαν καὶ ἔπεμψας τὸ ἅγιόν σου πνεῦμα ἀπὸ ὑπίστων. ("Who has known your counsel unless you have given wisdom and sent your spirit of holiness from on high?") The use of "spirit of holiness" in these texts is a synonym for the term "spirit of insight" (πνεῦμα συνέσεως) in Sir. 39:6 (see also 48:12, 24).

67. See M. Philonenko, "'Que ton esprit saint vienne sur nous et qu'il nous purifie' (Luc 11,2): l'arrière-plan qoumrânien d'une variante lucanienne du 'Notre Père,'" *Revue d'histoire et de philosophie religieuses* 75 (1995): 61–66.

6

GUIDED BY GOD

DIVINE AID IN INTERPRETATION
IN THE DEAD SEA SCROLLS
AND THE NEW TESTAMENT

R. Glenn Wooden

The New Testament has numerous citations of Old Testament passages because the Greek translations of the Hebrew Scriptures, the Septuagint translations, were the Bible of the early church.[1] However, there are a few places where the Old Testament texts are interpreted in ways that do not seem to be logical. For example, in Matthew 2:14–15 we read how Hosea 11:1 is a prediction of Jesus's return from Egypt as a baby:

1. For a convenient overview of the citations, see Steve Moyise, *The Old Testament in the New: An Introduction* (Continuum Biblical Studies Series; London/New York: Continuum, 2001).

Then Joseph got up, took the child and his mother by night, and went to Egypt, and remained there until the death of Herod. This was to fulfill what had been spoken by the Lord through the prophet, "Out of Egypt I have called my son."[2]

Consideration of the passage in Hosea, however, leaves us to wonder how there could be a relationship (Hos. 11:1–2, 5):

> When Israel was a child, I loved him,
>   and out of Egypt I called my son.
> The more I called them,[3]
>   the more they went from me;
> they kept sacrificing to the Baals,
>   and offering incense to idols.
> . . . .
> They shall return to the land of Egypt,
>   and Assyria shall be their king,
>   because they have refused to return to me.

In the context of the book of Hosea the most natural way to read "out of Egypt I called my son" is as a reference to the exodus of the people of Israel from Egypt, which is clear from the following material, especially 11:5, where the reference is made to the undoing of it, that is, to Israel returning to Egypt (although Egypt becomes Assyria). But Matthew understands "my son" as a reference to Jesus as a child and not to Israel as a child.

Again, just a few verses along, in Matthew 2:17–18, the prophecy from Jeremiah 31:15 is read as a prophecy of Herod's killing of the baby boys under the age of two years:

Then was fulfilled what had been spoken through the prophet Jeremiah:
> "A voice was heard in Ramah,
>   wailing and loud lamentation,
> Rachel weeping for her children;
>   she refused to be consoled, because they are no more."

2. Unless otherwise stated, all Scripture translations are from the NRSV.
3. The singulars "child," "him," and "son" refer to the nation Israel as an individual. In the next verse the focus moves from the corporate to the individual and thus to the use of plurals "them" and "they." The same happens in 11:3.

Jeremiah 31:15, however, is not a prophecy about the death of children in the future; it is about the lonely land of Judah longing for the return of its children, who are off in the land of Babylon, in exile—a return that the Lord promises will happen (Jer. 31:15–17):

> Thus says the LORD:
> A voice is heard in Ramah,
>   lamentation and bitter weeping.
> Rachel is weeping for her children;
>   she refuses to be comforted for her children,
>   because they are no more.
> Thus says the LORD:
> Keep your voice from weeping,
>   and your eyes from tears;
> for there is a reward for your work,
>   says the LORD:
>   they shall come back from the land of the enemy;
> there is hope for your future,
>   says the LORD:
> your children shall come back to their own country.

It is difficult for students of the Bible who are trained to interpret the text in its historical and literary contexts not to notice that these uses of the Old Testament are problematic. How could the writers of the New Testament Scriptures violate the plain meaning of the text in this way? The difficulties are clear, and the answers given are not always helpful.[4] In this exploration of the issue we will look at this practice in the broader context of the times and will find that it was an accepted interpretive practice leading up to the New Testament times, one that God used in the development of the New Testament Scriptures.

4. For example, Walter Kaiser's explanations do not deal with the issues here; *The Uses of the Old Testament in the New* (Chicago: Moody, 1985), 47–53. It is clear that Matthew cites Hosea because Jesus is the "son" and the going "down" to Egypt, where Hosea is cited in Matthew, is the preparation for the coming "out of" Egypt to which there is allusion just before the citation: "He was there until the death of Herod in order that what was spoken . . . might be fulfilled" (my translation). The story makes the connections to the cited text clear, and it is a fulfillment. Kaiser does, however, illustrate the difficulty of the passages, both by his own admission of the difficulties and because he attempts to show how the citations do not disregard the context from which they are taken (53).

What we find in interpretations such as Matthew's is not far removed from the practices used in a group of writings called the pesharim among the Dead Sea Scrolls.[5] The word *pesher* is merely a Hebrew and Aramaic word, פשר (*pešer*), brought into English without translation (*pesharim* is the Hebrew plural form), meaning "interpretation, meaning, explanation." In a work such as the pesher on the book of Habakkuk (1QpHab), the interpreter links everything to his own day, not to the time of the prophet, or to some as yet future time. It was believed by the author of the pesher, and presumably by the circle of the faithful for whom he was writing, that Habakkuk did not write about events in the prophet's own day, but rather about the distant future time of the pesherist. In the pesherist's scheme, the Chaldeans/Babylonians referred to in the book of Habakkuk were not the people from the Babylonian Empire of the sixth century BCE, but were the enemies of the true Israel in the second-century BCE writer's day, the Kittim, who were most probably the Romans.[6] He also finds other individuals and groups from his time in Habakkuk.

As an example of this method of interpretation, or better yet exposition, we will consider what the Habakkuk pesher says about Habakkuk 1:13. Before this verse God had told Habakkuk that as a response to the problem of unrighteousness

5. The extant pesharim cover the biblical books of Genesis (4Q252–54), Isaiah (3Q4; 4Q161–65), Hosea (4Q166–67), Micah (1Q14; 4Q168?), Nahum (4Q169), Habakkuk (1QpHab), Zephaniah (1Q15; 4Q170), Malachi (5Q10?), and Psalms (1Q16; 4Q171; 4Q173). Unless otherwise stated, all Dead Sea Scrolls translations are from Florentino García Martínez and Eibert J. C. Tigchelaar, *The Dead Sea Scrolls: Study Edition* (2 vols.; Leiden: Brill/Grand Rapids: Eerdmans, 1997–98). For a good introduction to the pesharim in general and to specific works, see Timothy H. Lim, *Pesharim* (Companion to the Qumran Scrolls 3; London: Sheffield Academic Press, 2002); and the following articles in *Encyclopedia of the Dead Sea Scrolls* (ed. L. H. Schiffman and J. C. VanderKam; 2 vols.; Oxford: Oxford University Press, 2000): Shani L. Berrin, "Pesharim" (2:644–47); George J. Brooke, "Genesis, Commentary on" (1:300–302); Moshe J. Bernstein, "Pesher Isaiah" (2:651–53); Moshe J. Bernstein, "Pesher Hosea" (2:650–51); Shani L. Berrin, "Pesher Nahum" (2:653–55); Moshe J. Bernstein, "Pesher Habakkuk" (2:647–50); and Moshe J. Bernstein, "Pesher Psalms" (2:655–56). A more technical treatment of the individual pesharim can be found in Maurya P. Horgan, *Pesharim: Qumran Interpretations of Biblical Books* (Catholic Biblical Quarterly Monograph Series 8; Washington, DC: Catholic Biblical Association, 1979).

6. Cf. Timothy H. Lim, "Kittim," in *Encyclopedia of the Dead Sea Scrolls* (ed. Schiffman and VanderKam), 1:469–71.

and violence about which the prophet was complaining, the Chaldeans would come to punish Israel. Habakkuk has a problem with this and reminds God about what he learned in his systematic theology course in the school of prophets: the Holy One cannot use a nation such as the Babylonians to punish the people of God:

> Your eyes are too pure to behold evil,
>   and you cannot look on wrongdoing;
> why do you [singular] look on the treacherous,
>   and are silent when the wicked swallow
>   those more righteous than they?

Although the prophet is lodging a complaint against the (in)action of God, using two sets of paired lines, the pesherist ignores the parallelism and interprets the statements as being addressed to two different groups of people in his day:

> "Your eyes are too pure to look at evil." Its interpretation [pesher]: they [God's chosen ones] have not run after the desire of their eyes in the era of wickedness. "Why do you [plural] stare, traitors, and remain silent when a wicked person consumes someone more upright than himself?" Its interpretation [pesher] concerns the House of Absalom and the members of their council, who kept silent when the Teacher of Righteousness was rebuked, and did not help him against the Man of the Lie, who rejected the Law in the middle of their whole Council. (1QpHab 5.6–12)

Instead of being a statement about the holiness of God, the first half of Habakkuk 1:13 becomes a statement about a group that was faithful to God, the followers of the Teacher of Righteousness. "You" in the second half of the verse is a plural in the pesher, the only difference between the singular and plural being one letter, ו (waw), at the end of the word.[7] It is applied to the "traitors"—which has changed from being what God "stares at" to being the ones addressed—in the time of the Teacher of Righteousness; they were people who did not speak up for the Teacher of Righteousness.

7. It is also possible that the pesherist found this in the text that was consulted.

In this interpretation of Habakkuk 1:13 the prophecy becomes disconnected from the days of Habakkuk, and the text is removed from any literary context within the book. This is similar to what we found in Matthew. It raises the question: how could they read texts in this way?

First, we need to remember that how we view the world today is not how it has always been viewed. Interpreting a portion of text by understanding it as much as possible in its context is a fundamental principle of reading today; it was not always so in the past, as the pesher on Habakkuk makes clear. And what is clear to us might not have been clear to others. This is, of course, the very phenomenon that separates groups today within the church and outside it; we read texts very differently because our contexts and experiences in life are different. However, the practice that we see in the scrolls and New Testament is dramatic. Nonetheless, the context and experiences of the Qumran covenanters and the early Christians allowed them to practice interpretation in ways that are foreign to us but seemed quite right to them.

Second, it is helpful for the reader to understand how these ancient interpreters seem to have understood what they were doing. This is where the remainder of this essay will focus: I want to consider the mind-set behind the techniques used in such interpretations, that is, the belief in divinely assisted interpretation.[8]

Since coming upon a discussion of the concept of "inspired interpretation" in Timothy Lim's book *Holy Scripture in the Qumran Commentaries and Pauline Letters*, I have been using the phrase to refer to the way in which Daniel interprets dreams, visions, and Scriptures in the book of Daniel.[9] I use it in parallel with "divinely assisted interpretation" because it is difficult to classify all the occurrences of interpretation under the same descriptor, especially since inspiration and an angel giving an interpretation are not quite the same.[10] Sometimes Daniel seems to be given an

8. On techniques, see Moshe J. Bernstein, "Interpretation of Scriptures," in *Encyclopedia of the Dead Sea Scrolls* (ed. Schiffman and VanderKam), 1:376–83; Berrin, "Pesharim"; and Lim, *Pesharim*.

9. Timothy H. Lim, *Holy Scripture in the Qumran Commentaries and Pauline Letters* (Oxford: Clarendon, 1997).

10. David Aune comments on this fuzzy use of the terms in his "Charismatic Exegesis in Early Judaism and Early Christianity," in *The Pseudepigrapha and*

internal divine ability (Dan. 1:17) that is recognized by others, such as in the story of Belshazzar, where it is commented that Daniel had in him "a spirit of holy gods" (5:11, 14). At other times he is assisted through night visions or visiting angels. From a scholarly point of view these are different kinds, and by talking about all of them under the same umbrella one could be accused of mixing categories or not neatly defining the types of religious phenomena; but clearly they were not viewed as being at odds with each other when the book of Daniel was finally composed, and from the point of view of that book "all roads lead to Jerusalem": the same God of Israel is the ultimate source of all of Daniel's abilities, visions, and angelic visitations.

Scholars use the descriptor "inspired interpretation" and a variety of similar ones to refer to the same set of beliefs, and the descriptors tend to be composed of two sets of related words: "inspired-charismatic-pneumatic" and "interpretation-exegesis."[11]

Early Biblical Interpretation (ed. J. H. Charlesworth and C. A. Evans; Journal for the Study of the Pseudepigrapha Supplement 14/Studies in Scripture in Early Judaism and Christianity 2; Sheffield: JSOT Press, 1993), 126.

11. On "inspired interpretation," see Lawrence H. Schiffman, *Reclaiming the Dead Sea Scrolls: The History of Judaism, the Background of Christianity, the Lost Library of Qumran* (Philadelphia: Jewish Publication Society, 1994), 225–26; Bernstein, "Pesher Habakkuk," 649; Daniel Patte, *Early Jewish Hermeneutic in Palestine* (Society of Biblical Literature Dissertation Series 22; Missoula, MT: Scholars Press, 1975), 201; Dieter Georgi, *The Opponents of Paul in Second Corinthians: A Study of Religious Propaganda in Late Antiquity* (trans. J. Riches; Philadelphia: Fortress, 1986), 111 (on Philo's "prophetically inspired" "exegetical activity"); Lim, *Holy Scripture*, 115–20, where he says that the Teacher of Righteousness "is an interpreter of biblical oracles, divinely inspired to be sure" (118); William M. Schniedewind, *The Word of God in Transition: From Prophet to Exegete in the Second Temple Period* (Journal for the Study of the Old Testament Supplement 197; Sheffield: Sheffield Academic Press, 1995), 128–29, 231, etc. On "inspired exegesis," see John R. Levison, *The Spirit in First Century Judaism* (Arbeiten zur Geschichte des antiken Judentums und des Urchristentums 29; Leiden: Brill, 1997), 257–59. On "charismatic exegesis," see William H. Brownlee, "Biblical Interpretation among the Sectaries of the Dead Sea Scrolls," *Biblical Archaeologist* 14 (1951): 61n4; David E. Aune, *Prophecy in Early Christianity and the Ancient Mediterranean World* (Grand Rapids: Eerdmans, 1983), 339–46; idem, "Charismatic Exegesis"; David E. Orton, *The Understanding Scribe: Matthew and the Apocalyptic Ideal* (Journal for the Study of the New Testament Supplement 25; Sheffield: JSOT Press, 1989), 118–19; Sze-kar Wan, "Charismatic Exegesis: Philo and Paul Compared," *Studia philonica* 6 (1994): 54–82; Levison, *Spirit in First Century Judaism*, 254–57. A variation of this is "pneumatic exegesis," on which see Matthias Henze, "The Narrative Frame of Daniel: A Literary Assessment,"

Basically, the idea is that instead of God giving new revelations, the existing records of revelations (Scriptures) became that through which the divine will was made known. Evidence of this belief is found in the Hebrew Bible itself. An important work by Michael Fishbane, *Biblical Interpretation in Ancient Israel*, shows how this is in evidence within the Hebrew Bible.[12] Also, the changing views of prophecy are in evidence in the books of 1–2 Chronicles, as William Schniedewind shows in his examination of prophecy and inspired interpretation in Israel in those books. He demonstrates how in Chronicles the title "prophet" is reserved for the classical prophets, who addressed the kings of Israel and Judah, and how "messenger" is reserved for those who came after the classical prophets, in times when there was no king, and who spoke to the people of God and interpreted the word of God to them.[13] Thus, the Bible itself shows that by the late biblical period, the move away from belief in the reception of new revelations to the reuse of existing ones had already begun to happen.

David Aune writes specifically on the topic of divinely aided interpretation and uses the descriptor "charismatic exegesis."[14] In his 1983 book he makes some very helpful clarifications of this approach to a text:

> "Charismatic exegesis," as now understood by biblical scholars, is . . . based on two presuppositions: (1) The sacred text contains

---

Journal for the Study of Judaism in the Persian, Hellenistic, and Roman Period 32 (2001): 8. On "charismatic interpretation," see Martin Hengel, *The Zealots: Investigations into the Jewish Freedom Movement in the Period from Herod I until 70 A.D.* (trans. D. Smith; Edinburgh: Clark, 1989), 234.

12. Michael Fishbane, *Biblical Interpretation in Ancient Israel* (Oxford: Clarendon, 1985). For a look at just one biblical book, see Katrina J. A. Larkin, *The Eschatology of Second Zechariah: A Study of the Formation of a Mantological Wisdom Anthology* (Contributions to Biblical Exegesis and Theology 6; Kampen, the Netherlands: Kok Pharos, 1994).

13. Schniedewind, *Word of God in Transition*, 80–129, 231–35. See especially the convenient chart on 234.

14. Aune's caution against using "inspired" is important; see "Charismatic Exegesis," 127–28. See Levison, *Spirit in First Century Judaism*, for a detailed examination of the belief in inspiration in the Hellenistic world and its influence on Jewish and Christian writers. His work *Of Two Minds: Ecstasy and Inspired Interpretation in the New Testament World* (Dead Sea Scrolls and Christian Origins Library 2; North Richland Hills: BIBAL, 1999) is a condensation of the larger work.

hidden or symbolic meanings which can only be revealed by an interpreter gifted with divine insight, and (2) The true meaning of the text concerns eschatological prophecies which the interpreter believes are being fulfilled in his own day. . . .

Charismatic exegesis . . . cannot be accurately characterized as either prophecy or divination. It resembles divination in that it deals with interpretation of coded messages, yet it is like prophecy in that the inspiration of the intermediary is involved.[15]

Aune follows this statement with four arguments that link "charismatic exegesis" more closely with divination, that is, the interpretation of divinely coded messages: (1) like divination it is indirect revelation, while prophecy is direct; (2) there is no trance; (3) this exegesis is dependent upon prophecies, and those prophecies continue to exist apart from the interpretations; and (4) there is a clear relationship between the interpretation of dreams, a practice of divination, and the charismatic exegesis of texts.[16] Nebuchadnezzar's dream in Daniel 2, Daniel's vision in chapter 7, and the interpretation of the prophecy from Jeremiah in Daniel 9 illustrate some of what Aune is saying. In Daniel 9, for example, Daniel is pondering the meaning of the prophecy of a seventy-year exile in the book of Jeremiah (25:11–12 and 29:10). An angel comes to him and interprets the prophecy, revealing from it information that no one would have thought was there from a contextual reading of the passages in Jeremiah. Seventy years was not meant, but seventy sevens, that is, seventy weeks of years:[17] "Seventy weeks are decreed for your people and your holy city: to finish the transgression, to put an end to sin, and to atone for iniquity, to bring in everlasting righteousness, to seal both vision and prophet, and to anoint a most holy place" (Dan. 9:24).

In relation to Aune's four points, we note the following: Daniel is visited by an angel while he is reading and praying; he does not receive completely new information but, rather, is given a new understanding of an existing prophecy; and the original

---

15. Aune, *Prophecy in Early Christianity*, 339; see also idem, "Charismatic Exegesis."

16. Aune, *Prophecy in Early Christianity*, 339–40.

17. Fishbane's consideration of this exegesis is helpful; *Biblical Interpretation in Ancient Israel*, 482–84.

prophecy remains in existence independent of the book of Daniel, as part of the book of Jeremiah. This has some clear similarities to what we find in the Dead Sea Scrolls.

The Dead Sea Scrolls

When we consider the interpretations of the Dead Sea Scrolls, there is no manual telling us how the interpreters did what they did or why they thought they could do it; there is no textbook for "Introduction to Peshering" at Essene College in Qumran. The pesher on Habakkuk, however, gives us a peek into the thought-world that legitimated their method of interpreting.

Twice in the *Habakkuk Pesher*, 2.1–10 and 7.1–8, we are told about the divine origins of the interpretive abilities of the Teacher of Righteousness.[18] The comments on Habakkuk 1:5 at 1QpHab 2.1–10 tell us that what he says comes "from the mouth of God" (2.2–3).[19] As well, he is "the Priest whom God has placed wi[thin the Commun]ity, to foretell the fulfilment of all the words of his servants, the prophets" (2.8–9).[20] In the comments on Habakkuk 2:2–3 at 1QpHab 7.1–8,[21] we learn that Habakkuk's vision, and indeed the prophecies of all the prophets,[22] had been filled by God with meaning for a future day, that God had made known to the Teacher of Righteousness that the day had come, and that

18. The following are well-rehearsed passages. Cf. Aune, "Charismatic Exegesis," 133–37; Lim, *Holy Scripture*, 118–20.

19. In 1Q22 2.6, the Mosaic law came "from the mouth of God"; and in 4Q377 frag. 1r 2.11, someone, presumably God, "spoke as an angel through his [Moses's] mouth."

20. Cf. 4Q381 frags. 76–77 line 8: "And you will pay attention to the wisdom which issues from my mouth."

21. 1QpHab 7.1–8: "God told Habakkuk to write what was going to happen <to> the last generation, but he did not let him know the consummation of the era. *Blank* And as for what he says: *Hab 2:2* 'So that /may run/ the one who reads it.' Its interpretation concerns the Teacher of Righteousness, to whom God has made known all the mysteries of the words of his servants, the prophets. *Hab 2:3* For the vision has an appointed time, it will have an end and not fail. *Blank* Its interpretation: the final age will be extended and go beyond all that the prophets say, because the mysteries of God are wonderful."

22. Cf. "and go beyond all that the prophets say" in 1QpHab 7.7–8. This sentence makes it clear that this same hermeneutic was to be applied to all of the prophets, and indeed it was applied to a variety of books, for which see 104n5 above.

God had revealed to the Teacher of Righteousness the significance of those prophecies. So here we have a divinely assisted interpreter of prophetic material, one who spoke the mysteries that came from the mouth of God, thus being able to make the connections to that writer's day and to bring out hidden meanings from the prophecies of old.

The writer(s) of the *Hodayot* (1QH[a]) also laid claim to revealed special knowledge about God and the mysteries of God.[23] The most explicit statement is found in 20.11–13: "And I, the Instructor [*maśkîl*], have known you, my God, through the spirit which you gave in me, and I have listened loyally to your wonderful secret through your holy spirit. You have [op]ened within me knowledge of the mystery of your wisdom, and the source of [your] power."[24]

Whether the writer(s) of the *Hodayot* were claiming prophetic or predictive abilities is unclear,[25] but they did claim that their

---

23. For an introduction to the *Hodayot*, see Émile Puech, "Hodayot," in *Encyclopedia of the Dead Sea Scrolls* (ed. Schiffman and VanderKam), 1:365–69.

24. In other locations the writer(s) gives thanks for the spirit that his God has placed in him or upon him; e.g., 1QH[a] 4.17: "[I give] you [thanks] for the spirits which you placed in me"; and 1QH[a] 4.26: "[I give thanks, because] you have spread [your] holy spirit upon your servant."

25. In the Hebrew Scriptures (e.g., Neh. 9:20), what came to people through the רוח ("spirit") of God was prophecies. Likewise in other Dead Sea Scrolls material: CD 2.12–13: "And he taught them by the hand of <the anointed ones> with his holy spirit and through seers of the truth, and their names were established with precision"; 1QS 8.16: "And according to what the prophets have revealed through his holy spirit"; and 4Q381 frag. 69 line 4: "And through his spirit prophets <were given> to you to teach you and show you." There are other claims of divinely revealed knowledge, such as 1QH[a] 6.8–11: "[Blessed are you,] Lord, who puts wisdom in the heart of [your] servant to kn[ow al]l these matters, to unders[tand. . . .] You teach your servant"; 1QH[a] 7.15: "But I, I know, thanks to your intellect"; 1QH[a] 9.21: "These things I know through your knowledge, for you opened my ears to wondrous mysteries although all I am is a creature of clay"; and 1QH[a] 19.27–28: "Blessed are yo[u, Lord,] because you have given [your] ser[vant] the insight of knowledge to understand your wonders." 1QH[a] 12.5–6 may also be a reference to special knowledge: "I give you thanks, Lord, because you have lightened my face for your covenant and [. . .] I have looked for you. Like perfect dawn you have revealed yourself to me with per[fect] light." Words for light are used in the Dead Sea Scrolls (as they are at Dan. 2:22 and 5:11) as wisdom terms. For example, 4Q511 frag. 18 2.7–8: "And I detest all deeds of impurity, for God made the knowledge of intelligence shine in my heart," to which compare 4Q511 frags. 48–49 + 51 line 1: "Because He has placed [the wisdom] of his intelligence [in my] hea[rt]";

knowledge of God and of the mysteries and power of God had come through a divine, indwelling spirit. This was not knowledge available to the common person or even to the average member of the writer's community.

In addition to the materials about the Teacher of Righteousness and the writer(s) of the *Hodayot*, at least one other Dead Sea Scrolls passage is relevant to this discussion, a composition about David, 11Q5 27.2–4, 11:

> And David, son of Jesse, was wise [חכם, *ḥākām*], and a light like the light of the sun, /and/ learned, *Blank* and discerning, and perfect in all his paths before God and men. And *Blank* YHWH gave him a discerning and enlightened spirit. And he wrote psalms. . . . All these he spoke through (the spirit of) prophecy which had been given to him from before the Most High.

Here the writer uses "wise," "light," "learned," "discerning," "enlightened," and "prophecy" to describe David; all but "prophecy" are found in the same or related form in the book of Daniel. This portrayal of David may be based upon passages such as 1 Samuel 18:14–15 (and 18:30, although this lone occurrence of the Qal verb is problematic), in which David is said to have been משכיל (*maśkîl*) and that YHWH was with him. Although probably intended to convey the idea of "successful," later interpreters might have understood משכיל with the more common sapiential denotation "insightful" or more likely with the religious force of special knowledge of God. Just as the plans for the temple in 1 Chronicles 28:19 were written out and David was helped in understanding (השכיל, *hiśkîl*) them by God, so in 11Q5 it is implied that the writing of the psalms was the result of the "discerning and enlightened spirit" that YHWH gave David, which is also described as נבואה (*nbw'h*, "prophesying") (27.11, translated as "[the spirit of] prophecy"). In this way David is like the prophet/seer Levites in Chronicles who prophesied when they sang.[26]

---

see also 11Q5 27.3. This understanding of light in 1QH[a] 12.5–6 seems to be confirmed in 12.27–28, where the writer also says that he teaches the many and passes on the "light" that he received from God.

26. 1 Chron. 25:1–7; 2 Chron. 20:14–21; 24:20; 25:15; 29:25–30; 34:30 (when compared to the parallel in 2 Kings 23:2, which has "prophets" instead of "Le-

Others made similar claims and give us some context in which to understand the Dead Sea Scrolls and New Testament practice of interpretation. We will consider two: Philo and Josephus.

Philo

Philo was a Jewish interpreter born around 20–15 BCE into a wealthy Jewish family in Alexandria, Egypt; he died in about 50 CE.[27] He wrote many works interpreting biblical texts, and he believed that he was divinely assisted in that task. In his book *On Dreams* (*De somniis*) he writes about hearing "the voice of the invisible spirit, the familiar secret tenant" that taught him "that there is a great and precious matter of which [he] knew nothing" (2.252).[28] In another book, *On Cherubim* (*De cherubim*), he writes, similarly: "But there is a higher thought than these. It comes from a voice in my own soul, which oftentimes is god-possessed and divines where it does not know. . . . The voice told me . . ." (27). Some of the significance of these autobiographical passages is made clear when we compare them with *On the Life of Moses* (*De vita Mosis*):

> Moses, when he heard of this [the manna] and also actually saw it, was awestruck and, guided by what was not so much surmise as *God-sent inspiration*, made announcement of the Sabbath. I need hardly say that *conjectures* of this kind are closely *akin to prophecies*. For the mind could not have made so straight an aim if there was not also the *divine spirit guiding it to the truth itself*. (2.264–65, emphasis added)

---

vites"; see the discussion by Schniedewind, *Word of God in Transition*, 184–86). On David, see Schniedewind, *Word of God in Transition*, 171–73, 189–208. On the Levites, see David L. Petersen, *Late Israelite Prophecy: Studies in Deutero-Prophetic Literature and in Chronicles* (Society of Biblical Literature Monograph Series 23; Missoula, MT: Scholars Press, 1977), 55–96; and especially Schniedewind, *Word of God in Transition*, 163–88.

27. For discussion of the following and other passages, see Levison, *Spirit in First Century Judaism* and *Of Two Minds*.

28. Philo translations are adapted from the Colson-Whitaker-Marcus translation in the Loeb Classical Library (*Philo: Works* [trans. F. H. Colson, G. H. Whitaker, and Ralph Marcus; 12 vols.; Cambridge: Harvard University Press; London: Heinemann, 1929–62]).

For Philo the divine spirit guided the mind of some humans, he being one, to make accurate conjectures about the significance of some events and about Scripture passages that were difficult to understand or that had hidden meaning.

Josephus

Josephus was born in 37 CE into a priestly Jewish family; he died in 100 CE.[29] In his lifetime he wrote two major histories of the Jewish people, a book about his own life, and another in which he refuted criticisms of Judaism by Hellenistic authors. In his works he also provides some reflection on how people could predict the future and gives some interesting examples of divinely assisted predictors. We are not concerned with the veracity of the accounts, their sources, or their relation to the Dead Sea Scrolls or the Qumran community, but rather with the portrayal itself.

Before considering the actual stories of the Essenes, it may be helpful to note the distinction that Josephus seems to maintain between the classical prophets and those who came after the time of Artaxerxes (*Against Apion* 1.41).[30] Although people after the time of Artaxerxes predicted the future, Josephus only once calls anyone but the biblical prophets by the title "prophet."[31] The reason would seem to be that, due to "the failure of the exact succession of the prophets" (*Against Apion* 1.41), there was no

29. Josephus translations are from the Thackeray-Marcus-Wikgren-Feldman translation in the Loeb Classical Library (*Josephus: Works* [trans. H. St. J. Thackeray, Ralph Marcus, Allen Wikgren, and L. H. Feldman; 13 vols.; Cambridge: Harvard Unviersity Press; London: Heinemann, 1926–65]). As is evident from the footnotes, I make significant use of Rebecca Gray, *Prophetic Figures in Late Second Temple Jewish Palestine: The Evidence from Josephus* (New York: Oxford University Press, 1993). For a critique of her work, see Steve Mason's review in *Ioudaios Review* 4.006.94 (http://listserv.lehigh.edu/lists/ioudaios-review/ir_index4.html#4.006).

30. Presumably this terminus is chosen in order to include Esther among the prophets; Louis H. Feldman, "Prophets and Prophecy in Josephus," *Journal of Theological Studies* 41 (1990): 386–422.

31. That person is Cleodemus, in *Antiquities* 1.240, although as Feldman points out, it is most likely a quotation from Alexander Polyhistor; "Prophets and Prophecy in Josephus," 400–401.

way to verify the credentials of one who might be a prophet. Not using the term "prophet" of someone who predicted the future was not, therefore, a matter of a lack of accuracy in predicting or of inspiration, but was due to a technical reason focused upon the passing of the office from prophet to student.[32] According to Josephus, however, prophecy in the sense of predicting the future did not cease, and those who practiced this art he calls mantics (μάντεις).[33] Among those who predict the future in the works of Josephus (himself included among them) are three Essenes: Judas, Menahem, and Simon.

Before considering the stories, it is important to consider a passage in which Josephus talks about these Essene predictors. In *Jewish War* 2.159 he explains how he understood such mantics to predict: "There are some among them [the Essenes] who profess to foretell the future, being versed from their early years in holy books, various forms of purification and apothegms of prophets; and seldom, if ever, do they err in their predictions."[34] Unfortunately, Josephus does not make clear how being educated in these three things helped in the prediction of the future and interpretation of dreams. In the stories, however, he says that

32. Ibid., 405; contra Gray, *Prophetic Figures*, 34, 109.

33. See Gray, *Prophetic Figures*, 107–10, for a discussion of the use of the μαντ- group of words by Josephus. One major flaw in her overall argument is the discussion of *Antiquities* 6.327, where Josephus relates how Saul had banished "the diviners [τοὺς μάντεις], ventriloquists and all practitioners of such arts, except the prophets [τῶν προφητῶν]." The point that Gray makes is that the word is here used "not to distinguish certain figures from genuine prophets, but rather to point to types of prophecy that required a certain degree of technical expertise" (110). (By "prophecy," she means "prediction.") It seems, however, that Josephus does just what she says he does not. Various types predicted the future ("practitioners"), but only those who were specially enabled to do so by God and who were verified as being in the prophetic tradition were allowed to stay. One who had predictive abilities but was outside the line of prophets could be called a μάντις ("mantic"), but not a προφήτης ("prophet"), since the source of the ability was not clearly attributable to God. Thus, Josephus makes a qualitative difference between μάντις and προφήτης. It has little to do with the "expression of a vague nostalgia that idealized the past as a time when people were, in some indescribable way, closer to God and holier than in the present" (34) or with some predictors being "really great" and others being "unworthy of the title" (109). See also Schniedewind's *Word of God in Transition* on the late biblical move away from the use of "prophet" for later biblical figures.

34. See Gray, *Prophetic Figures*, 83–92, for commentary and bibliography on this passage. See also Lim, *Holy Scripture*, 114.

"many of these men have indeed been vouchsafed a knowledge of divine things because of their virtue" (*Antiquities* 15.379). There seems, therefore, to be a requirement that those who predict the future be knowledgeable about Scriptures and prophetic materials and to be ritually pure or virtuous.[35]

Of the three stories of Essenes who predicted accurately, we will consider the one about Judas in *Jewish War* 1.78–80 and *Antiquities* 13.311–13.[36] The story relates how this mantic had predicted that Antigonus would die on a particular day at a location named Strato's Tower. When on that day Antigonus and his troops passed where Judas was teaching his disciples at the temple in Jerusalem, it was clear to Judas that Antigonus was too far from the predicted location; thus he was distressed because he had apparently given a false prediction. However, Josephus relates that Antigonus was killed on that day at a different location by the same name, thus saving the reputation of Judas. For our purposes there are two interesting features in this story. First is the specificity of the prediction: Judas had predicted that a specific individual, Antigonus, was going to die on a specific day, the one on which Judas saw Antigonus, and that it would take place at a specific place, Strato's Tower. This was not a general sort of prediction that could be fulfilled by just any event.

35. Cf. Gray, *Prophetic Figures*, 86–88, 105. When Josephus refers in *Antiquities* 13 to Onias's desire to build a temple in Egypt, Onias—another person who predicts the future—resorts to a prophecy of Isaiah that had not been fulfilled as the basis for his going ahead with the building of the temple: "In this desire he was encouraged chiefly by the words of the prophet Isaiah, who had lived more than six hundred years before and had foretold that a temple to the Most High God was surely to be built in Egypt by a Jew. . . . For this indeed is what the prophet Isaiah foretold, 'There shall be an altar in Egypt to the Lord God,' and many other such things did he prophesy concerning this place" (*Antiquities* 13.64, 68). In a similar way, Ben Sira, in his description of the scribe, connects the study of the writings with purity of life: "How different the one who devotes himself to the study of the law of the Most High! He seeks out the wisdom of all the ancients, and is concerned with prophecies. . . . He sets his heart to rise early to seek the Lord who made him, and to petition the Most High; he opens his mouth in prayer and asks pardon for his sins" (Sir. 38:34b–39:1, 5).

36. The two other stories are about Menahem, who predicted the rise of Herod to king, when Herod was still a boy (*Antiquities* 15.373–79), and Simon, who interpreted a dream for Archelaus (*Jewish War* 2.111–13; *Antiquities* 17.345–48).

Second, we are told that Judas had a large number of acquaintances whom he was instructing in how to tell the future: "He exclaimed to his acquaintances—a considerable number of his disciples were seated beside him" (*Jewish War* 1.78)—and "cried out to his companions and disciples, who were together with him for the purpose of receiving instruction in foretelling the future" (*Antiquities* 13.311). How he was teaching them to do this is not evident from the passage, but given the link that Josephus makes elsewhere to the study of the sacred books and the sayings of the prophets, and to living a virtuous/pure life, Judas may have been instructing his students in these. However, given the specificity of the prediction in Judas's case, how this would be based simply upon the sacred writings or the prophets is in no way clear.[37] From other things that he says, however, it is clear that the ability to predict is attributed to God, which makes it likely that he was teaching the disciples how to be prepared should God choose one of them to use for this purpose.

Besides the three Essenes, Josephus also claimed that he himself was divinely assisted in predicting future events. In *Life* 208 he speaks of how one night it seemed to him that someone stood by his bed and spoke to him, reassuring him about his safety and future.[38] In *Jewish War* 3.351–54 he refers back to this event and classes it among the "ambiguous utterances of the Deity." As well, in this same passage he seems to ascribe his own ability to interpret and to predict the future to his knowledge of "the prophecies [contained] in the sacred books" and to his being a priest and of priestly lineage. These priestly connections, among other things, are a possible suggestion of his purity. In this passage he also claims to have been in a state of ecstasy in which he talked with God about the dreams. Just a little further on, in 3.405–6, when he actually tells what it was that he predicted,[39]

---

37. See also, Gray, *Prophetic Figures*, 94, 105–7.

38. "That night I beheld a marvellous vision in my dreams. I had retired to my couch, grieved and distraught by the tidings in the letter, when I thought that there stood by me one who said: 'Cease, man, from your sorrow of heart, let go all fear.'"

39. According to rabbinic tradition the one who made the prediction was Rabbi Yohanan ben Zakkai; Emil Schürer, *The History of the Jewish People in the Age of Jesus Christ (175 B.C.–A.D. 135)* (rev. and ed. Geza Vermes et al.; 2nd ed.; Edinburgh: Clark, 1973–87), 1:494n41.

the specificity is like that of the prediction made by Judas: the inhabitants of Jotapata would be captured on the forty-seventh day, and Josephus would be caught alive by the Romans. Again, these are hardly vague predictions that could be fulfilled by just any events, and they are predictions that do not have an obvious basis in prophetic materials. He wants us to conclude that they are of divine origins.

In this period, then, we find various pious Jews who portrayed themselves, or who were portrayed, as having interpreted the prophets or dreams or predicted the future *through divine assistance*. In all these cases the predictions or interpretations go well beyond what biblical texts say; these individuals must have believed that they were able to extract the mysteries of God from the text or dreams through various kinds of divine assistance.

New Testament

Let us now come back to the New Testament. There is some disagreement about whether early Christians such as Paul thought of themselves as being divinely assisted or inspired as they wrote. The techniques used in some books of the New Testament do have similarities to those found in the Dead Sea Scrolls, however. And there are some indications that it was believed that, if not the writers of the books, then the Christian communities generally were divinely assisted in their understanding of the things of God. For example, in the Johannine writings, we hear Jesus say to the disciples: "When the Spirit of truth comes, he will guide you into all the truth; for he will not speak on his own, but will speak whatever he hears, and he will declare to you the things that are to come" (John 16:13). And we hear a Johannine congregation counseled as follows: "As for you, the anointing that you received from him abides in you, and so you do not need anyone to teach you. But as his anointing teaches you about all things, and is true and is not a lie, and just as it has taught you, abide in him" (1 John 2:27). It is important here not to read either of these in an individualistic way. "You" is plural in the Greek, and so the admonition is to groups. How this would be manifested in the group is unclear, but it is likely that it is through teachers who are part of the congregation.

Paul says similar things in 1 Corinthians 2:6–13:

> Yet among the mature we do speak wisdom, though it is not a wisdom of this age or of the rulers of this age, who are doomed to perish. But we speak God's wisdom, secret and hidden [cf. Dan. 2:20–22], which God decreed before the ages for our glory. None of the rulers of this age understood this; for if they had, they would not have crucified the Lord of glory. . . . These things God has revealed to us through the Spirit; for the Spirit searches everything, even the depths of God [cf. Dan. 2:22]. For what human being knows what is truly human except the human spirit that is within? So also no one comprehends what is truly God's except the Spirit of God. Now we have received not the spirit of the world, but the Spirit that is from God, so that we may understand the gifts bestowed on us by God. And we speak of these things in words not taught by human wisdom but taught by the Spirit, interpreting spiritual things to those who are spiritual.

And similarly in the prayer in Ephesians 1:17–18 we read: "I pray that the God of our Lord Jesus Christ, the Father of glory, may give you a spirit of wisdom and revelation as you come to know him, so that, with the eyes of your heart enlightened, you may know what is the hope to which he has called you."

We need to be clear that the New Testament writers were not connected to the Qumran community in a genetic way. Aune rightfully disputes seeing the New Testament passages just cited as suggesting that the early church consciously practiced charismatic exegesis. They do not refer to the interpretation of Scripture, only to the reception of divine wisdom through the aid of the Spirit of God. However, what we find in these passages is consistent with what we find in the other nonbiblical writings that do make such claims or give examples of it. The early church, interpreting the prophecy of Joel for its day, saw the Spirit of God as being given to all Christians, and thus, in the passages quoted from the Johannine and Pauline materials, it is not only special teachers who know the truth or receive wisdom and revelation, it is everyone! As Aune rightly observes, the issue is complex. However, it seems clear that knowing about the practice of inspired, or divinely aided, interpretation puts the New Testament practices into a helpful light.

So, back to Matthew. Matthew believed that Jesus was the key to unlocking the Jewish Scriptures, the Bible of the early church. He found Jesus in his Scriptures, and in a cultural context that allowed for the kind of interpretive approach for which we find evidence in the pesharim, Philo, and Josephus, he could consider an event in the life of Christ and point to prophecies in Hosea and Jeremiah and say, "See, here is a prophecy about that event in the life of Jesus!"[40] And that was quite acceptable, because people knew that God had hidden in the Scriptures meanings that were not obvious to the unaided interpreter. But to one in whom was the Spirit of God, all could become clear.

40. See Adam S. van der Woude, "Prophetic Prediction, Political Prognostication, and Firm Belief: Reflections on Daniel 11:40–12:3," in *The Quest for Context and Meaning: Studies in Biblical Intertextuality in Honor of James A. Sanders* (ed. C. A. Evans and S. Talmon; Biblical Interpretation Series 28; Leiden: Brill, 1997), 63–73.

7

THE DEAD SEA SCROLLS AND CHRISTIAN THEOLOGY

Jonathan R. Wilson

The title of this book is *The Dead Sea Scrolls and Christian Origins*. My presence as a theologian and the topic of my chapter immediately raise questions: What do the Dead Sea Scrolls have to do with Christian theology? What is a theologian doing in the middle, or rather at the end, of all these Bible scholars and historians of early Christianity? Certainly the scrolls have a bearing on our understanding of one trajectory of the development of the history of God's people as told in the Old Testament. And certainly the scrolls have a significant contribution to make to our understanding of the New Testament. At least, I expect that readers will have been convinced of these claims by the essays in the present volume. But Christian theology? Is not the first act of interpretation the work of the biblical scholars, who determine what the text meant? Should not the theologians be waiting in the wings for later acts—perhaps act 2, but possibly even act 3? In this scenario, act 2 would be the summary of the exegetes' work by biblical theology, and act 3 would be the work of the theologians in systematizing, categorizing, turning the earlier material into doctrines.[1] The questions and confusions that I playfully identify are also real questions and confusions. They have been with us for some time now. In some settings they have been well worked over and resolved. In other settings they have not. In any setting, they are worth returning to, so I am going to begin by drawing them out a bit further and offering a resolution—an *apologia pro theologia* (defense of theology). Then, having identified myself with an understanding of how we Christians submit ourselves to our textual traditions, I will address to my colleagues one matter of doctrinal concern. Finally, I will develop that doctrinal concern one step further to explore what I consider an absolutely critical (in the sense of essential) question about the future trajectory of the life of God's people in northern European and, more narrowly, northern American society.

In order to explore the questions related to the role of theology in textual interpretation, I will develop, in place of my earlier playful imagery, the image of a relay race.[2] After I develop the image I will argue that it seriously misleads us. In its place I will suggest a more appropriate practice to guide our work together.

Instead of theologians waiting in the wings for act 3, imagine theologians on a racetrack, waiting in the passing zone to run the third leg of a relay race. The first leg of the race is run by the exegetes, who then pass the baton of "the meaning of the text" to the biblical theologians for the second leg of the race. At the end of the second leg the biblical theologians pass the baton of "what it meant" on to the theologians, who run the third leg of the race and pass the baton of "what it means" to pastors, who run the fourth leg of the relay and pass the baton of "how it applies" to their congregations.

Now imagine the problems with this account of textual fidelity. We can well imagine the exegetes, instead of staying in their lanes and running a straightforward race, beginning to argue

1. The fullest development of this dramatic imagery for the work of theology is Nicholas Lash, *Theology on the Way to Emmaus* (London: SCM, 1986), 37–46.
2. Like the earlier image, this one is most fully developed by Lash, ibid., 75–92. The account here was developed independent of Lash, though it is nearly identical.

among themselves about which baton to pass on. We can imagine the biblical theologians falling into disagreement over "what it meant." In the meantime, the theologians, not to mention the pastors, are waiting in the passing zone to run their leg of the race—which never gets run. Or we may imagine six different exegetes or biblical theologians arriving at the passing zone. Which baton do I, as a theologian, receive? But the problems with this practice are deeper than the practical or logistical.

This scenario reflects the account of contemporary biblical theology by Krister Stendahl.[3] Stendahl's account has been subjected to much criticism.[4] Although the deficiencies in Stendahl's account are now widely recognized, the practices that he describes maintain a significant grip on us. These practices tend to conceal the interpretive interests already operative in exegesis, the theological convictions that underwrite a claim simply to be studying history, and the place of one's calling in the church. They maintain their grip on us because of our own acquiescence and because we have institutionalized them in commentary series and in seminary and graduate school curricula.

But the tide has turned. In many seminaries and graduate programs, Bible scholars and theologians are working to dismantle the wall of separation. Two commentary series that I know of are doing the same: Two Horizons (edited by Joel Green et al.) and Brazos Theological Commentary on the Bible (edited by R. R. Reno et al.). The corrective represented by these developments recognizes that textual fidelity requires the skills, questions, and contributions of all of us at a variety of stages. We are a team, let's say a basketball team, working together toward a common goal. We have different skills and different responsibilities, but we are always working together—not just theologians, exegetes, and historians, but also pastors, counselors, chaplains, lawyers, farmers, parents, and so on.

3. The classic statement of this formula is Krister Stendahl, "Biblical Theology, Contemporary," in *The Interpreter's Dictionary of the Bible* (ed. G. A. Buttrick et al.; New York: Abingdon, 1962), 1:418–32.

4. For a fuller consideration of these problems, see Ben C. Ollenburger, "What Krister Stendahl Meant—A Normative Critique of Descriptive Biblical Theology," *Horizons in Biblical Theology* 8 (1986): 61–98; and Stephen E. Fowl, *Engaging Scripture: A Model for Theological Interpretation* (Oxford: Blackwell, 1998), 13–21.

To return to the specific question that began our journey, theologians do not simply wait for the deliverances of the exegetes and biblical theologians; they also suggest agenda items. They may also challenge and identify doctrinal assumptions and conclusions drawn by exegetes. Of course, the contrary is also the case. Bible scholars may suggest, even urge, an agenda item upon theologians.

To see how this might work out in practice, let us turn to an issue of some concern for us all on which we may find some guidance through our reading of the Dead Sea Scrolls. Recently, the term "apocalyptic" has become significant for our thinking. For several years, some biblical exegetes have been attending to a dimension of the Bible that they label "apocalyptic." At the same time, some theologians make use of this category to shape their own theologies. And since the terrorist attacks at the World Trade Center, commentators have been using "apocalyptic" to describe the times in which we live.

For Christians, of course, the scrolls do not teach authoritatively. But do they not portray for us a community whose apocalyptic vision of the world contributes to our understanding of apocalyptic in the Bible? And then by extension, may they also contribute to understanding our own apocalyptic vision?

Although the past years have seen a rise in the use of apocalyptic in many places, these various uses have only recently been brought together by Canadian Baptist theologian Douglas Harink.[5] In his book *Paul among the Postliberals*, Harink devotes one chapter, "Apocalypse," to reading together Stanley Hauerwas, Galatians, and New Testament scholars J. Louis Martyn and Richard Hays, in the middle of our cultural moment. Identifying "apocalypse" as "shorthand for Jesus Christ," Harink argues that

> in the New Testament, in particular for Paul, all apocalyptic reflection and hope comes to this, that God has acted critically, decisively, and finally for Israel, all the peoples of the earth, and the entire cosmos, in the life, death, resurrection, and coming again of Jesus, in such a way that God's purpose for Israel, all humanity,

5. Douglas Harink, *Paul among the Postliberals: Pauline Theology beyond Christendom and Modernity* (Grand Rapids: Brazos, 2003), chap. 2.

and all creation is critically, decisively, and finally disclosed and effected in the history of Jesus Christ.[6]

This means, then, that "apocalyptic theology is theology 'without reserve,' that is, theology which leaves no reserve of space or time or concept or aspect of creation outside of or beyond or undetermined by the critical decisive, final action of God in Jesus Christ."[7]

As Harink explores this apocalyptic theology, particularly in Hauerwas, he exposes the ways that liberal societies domesticate the apocalyptic gospel by turning it into religion. In resistance to that domestication we need an apocalyptic theology that begins and ends with God's action in the history of Jesus, that recognizes the cosmic conflict with enslaving powers and the intrinsically political nature of the gospel, that rejects the privatization of Christian faith and the "hegemony of secular social-scientific rationality,"[8] and that recognizes the necessity of God's invasive work in the cosmos as the decisive judgment that redeems through the powerful suffering of Jesus Christ.

Such an understanding, according to Harink, stands over against much New Testament scholarship and Christian theology. In New Testament studies, this apocalyptic perspective resists the work of E. P. Sanders, J. D. G. Dunn, and N. T. Wright because their "new perspectives" remain too indebted to social-scientific categories such as "boundaries" and "inclusion and exclusion" and "are insufficiently apocalyptic/theological."[9] In Christian theology, this apocalyptic vision calls for a totalizing theology that reflects not the arrogance of the theologian or the *imperium* of theology but the convictions we have about the apocalypse—the showing and the doing—which is Jesus Christ and the way in which we participate in that apocalypse.

In the contemporary context and the many uses of apocalyptic, two points are crucial. First, the showing and doing that is the apocalypse of Jesus Christ finds its center in the cross, which simultaneously reveals the evil of this age and God's redemption

6. Ibid., 68.
7. Ibid., 69.
8. Ibid., 75.
9. Ibid., 71. The full text acknowledges "the element of truth in these and similar construals."

of the cosmos. This cross, however, stands in the middle of the history that is Israel's and, through Christ, also ours. That is to say, to get Christian apocalyptic right we must learn the history that is named by Israel and the church in light of the crucifixion of Jesus Christ. Second, this apocalyptic vision carries with it a certainty about the conflict between good and evil that is lived out by way of suffering discipleship. The victory in this war belongs to "the Lamb that was slain."[10]

These apocalyptic claims have particular poignancy for the life of the church today. In the next section I will turn directly to that subject. Here I want simply to ask my colleagues who read these texts from the Qumran community what light the scrolls might shed on this call to apocalyptic theology. Do these texts shed light on the notion of Paul as apocalyptic theologian? Do they provide us with another apocalyptic vision on which we could reflect critically and appreciatively? In what ways are the scrolls also totalizing theology that brings all of life under the decisive judgment of God's action in history?

As I noted above, the fullest engagement with apocalyptic comes within the context of the concrete shape of the life of the community. Since apocalyptic is not just a showing but also a doing, the question of the manner of our participation in the apocalypse of Jesus Christ brings our talk to its decisive point: how shall we live? One possible consequence of apocalyptic theology (perhaps the most natural) is withdrawal from society by the apocalyptic community. And it is here that the community of the scrolls engages and challenges the church today.

To bring this engagement into focus, I return to Harink's quint-essential apocalyptic theologian, Stanley Hauerwas. One of the most forceful criticisms directed toward Hauerwas is the accusation of "sectarianism."[11] This accusation is meant to convey

---

10. The most mature and influential account of this claim is John Howard Yoder, *The Politics of Jesus: Vicit Agnus Noster* (2nd ed.; Grand Rapids: Eerdmans, 1994).

11. This accusation may be found in James M. Gustafson, "The Sectarian Temptation: Reflections on Theology, the Church, and the University," *Proceedings of the Catholic Theological Society* 40 (1985): 83–94; and Max L. Stackhouse, "Liberalism Dispatched vs. Liberalism Engaged," *Christian Century* (Oct. 18, 1985): 962–67. For further reflections on sectarianism, see Philip D. Kenneson, *Beyond Sectarianism: Re-imagining Church and World* (Valley Forge, PA: Trinity, 1999); and Robert H. Gundry, *Jesus the Word according to John the Sectarian: A*

the conviction that Hauerwas's apocalyptic theology suppresses a fundamental liberal dynamic in Christianity, denies the goodness of creation, endorses a strategic withdrawal from the life of the world, and ends in an irrational fideism.

Hauerwas and others have responded at length to these accusations. Their responses have not resolved the controversy, nor have they really advanced the debate beyond recognizing that two fundamentally different paradigms are at work. It is as if the two sides are using the same vocabulary to speak different languages. On these matters I stand closer to Hauerwas than to his accusers. The issues are difficult to explicate briefly because they require us to break out of familiar habits of thinking and living. In this contemporary apocalyptic theology, Western liberalism denies the truth of Jesus Christ because it imagines us to be individual units of desire who must develop ways of sharing space and time without restricting one another's freedoms unnecessarily. Compare this to the church as central to the gospel. In apocalyptic theology, the goodness of creation cannot be affirmed, as the accusers desire, independently of the work of Jesus Christ on behalf of creation. Creation is good, but only in Christ. The strategy of withdrawing from society is a temptation for apocalyptic theology, but is it an inevitable consequence? Hauerwas himself certainly models cultural engagement, not withdrawal; the life of the church is fully engaged in the life of this world because it is the life of the church that bears witness to the world of the one decisive act on its behalf in Jesus Christ. In apocalyptic theology the church bears witness to Christ's lordship not through the weapons of this world but by identification with the suffering Messiah, whose life, death, resurrection, and coming again is the hope of the world.

Such response and clarification are important in our present context. But my concern here is not to decide or even debate the accusation of sectarianism directed toward Hauerwas. Rather, my interest lies in drawing us into the kind of conversation I imagined earlier. In light of the supposed connection between apocalyptic theology and sectarianism, whether in Hauerwas or elsewhere, what may the scrolls and the community that pro-

---

Paleofundamentalist Manifesto for Evangelicalism, especially Its Elites, in North America (Grand Rapids: Eerdmans, 2002).

duced them teach those of us who adopt an apocalyptic theology today?

At the end of his seminal work *After Virtue*, Alasdair MacIntyre asserts that unlike the rise of the first monastic movement in Christianity, when the barbarians were at the gates, today "the barbarians are already among us and have been for sometime. So we await not Godot but another—doubtless very different—St. Benedict."[12] That statement itself is apocalyptic in tone and intent. As many are convinced by MacIntyre's argument, the question arises, "What would this new monasticism look like?"[13]

Is Qumran (i.e., the scrolls and the community that produced them and whose life is reflected in them) an instance of a monastic or semimonastic community that withdrew from the larger society? Or are the familiar characterizations of Qumran, like those directed toward Hauerwas as a sectarian, the consequence of incommensurable paradigms? Is Qumran an instance of sectarian withdrawal as a consequence of apocalyptic theology? If so, what characteristics of their apocalypticism effected this withdrawal? If not, what interrupted that movement or protected them from it? As some of us adopt apocalyptic theology and reflect on the possibilities and shape of a new monasticism, but also desire to avoid those errors gathered, perhaps unfairly, under the accusation of sectarianism, in what ways might our predecessors at Qumran speak to us today?

12. Alasdair MacIntyre, *After Virtue: A Study in Moral Theory* (South Bend: University of Notre Dame Press, 1984), 263.

13. I explore this question in a preliminary way in Jonathan R. Wilson, *Living Faithfully in a Fragmented World: Lessons from the Church for MacIntyre's "After Virtue"* (Valley Forge, PA: Trinity, 1997). For further development, see The Rutba House, ed., *School(s) for Conversion: 12 Marks of a New Monasticism* (Eugene, OR: Cascade Books, 2005).

8

APOCALYPTIC THEOLOGY AND THE DEAD SEA SCROLLS

A RESPONSE TO JONATHAN WILSON

John J. Collins

Jonathan Wilson raises some important issues in his essay and addresses some specific questions to those of us who work primarily with the ancient texts. I would like to offer a brief response to these questions.

As Wilson notes, interdisciplinary work is difficult in the modern age of specialized scholarship. It is difficult enough to keep abreast of developments in one's own field, let alone become competent in another discipline. Both biblical studies and theology are contested fields. In each, there are many incompatible paradigms claiming our allegiance. Even scholars who engage seriously in interdisciplinary dialogue often pick just one paradigm as dialogue partner, because they happen to be familiar with it or find it congenial. Those who find the selected paradigm deficient are not likely to be impressed by the fruit of the resulting interdisciplinary dialogue.

From my perspective as a longtime student of ancient apocalyptic writings, including the Dead Sea Scrolls,[1] the postliberal paradigm, based though it is on the work of such reputable scholars as J. Louis Martyn and Richard Hays, is seriously deficient, because it focuses on one very specific kind of apocalypticism (that of Paul) and dismisses the great bulk of ancient apocalyptic literature as irrelevant. (The author of the introductory article in the Martyn Festschrift declares that much of the genre is "abstruse and fantastic.")[2] Such an approach may seem attractive to theologians who are thereby dispensed from the labor of deciphering the books of *Enoch* or the Dead Sea Scrolls, but it loses sight of the context within which Pauline and all Christian apocalypticism developed. The loss is compounded if one rejects the use of social-scientific categories out of hand, as it is difficult if not impossible to compare different religious systems without some use of such categories.

In fact, of course, Paul's apocalyptic vision was one among many. This is recognized implicitly in Wilson's question whether the scrolls provide us with another apocalyptic vision on which we could reflect. If "apocalypse" were identified as "shorthand for Jesus Christ," as Harink would have it, then Wilson's question would have to be answered in the negative. If apocalypse is identified either as a literary genre or as a particular structure of thought, however, then Wilson's question becomes fruitful. In order to answer it, however, we must reflect for a moment on what makes any vision apocalyptic.

The words "apocalypse" and "apocalyptic" are derived from the Greek word for revelation, *apokalypsis*. The ancient Jewish and Christian texts that are called apocalypses are identified first of all because they report revelations of a distinctly otherworldly character.[3] Typically, they report either symbolic visions (as in

---

1. See my books *The Apocalyptic Imagination* (2nd ed.; Grand Rapids: Eerdmans, 1998) and *Apocalypticism in the Dead Sea Scrolls* (London: Routledge, 1997). See also B. McGinn, J. J. Collins, and S. Stein, eds., *The Encyclopedia of Apocalypticism* (3 vols.; New York: Continuum, 1998).

2. R. Sturm, "Defining the Word 'Apocalyptic,'" in *Apocalyptic and the New Testament: Essays in Honor of J. Louis Martyn* (ed. J. Marcus and M. L. Soards; Journal for the Study of the New Testament Supplement 24; Sheffield: Sheffield Academic Press, 1989), 37.

3. On the identification of ancient apocalypses, see J. J. Collins, ed., "Apocalypse: The Morphology of a Genre," *Semeia* 14 (1979). The centrality of revelation

Dan. 7–12 or Revelation) or otherworldly journeys (as in some of the writings attributed to Enoch or the Christian apocalypses of Peter and Paul), which are explained to the visionary by an angel. All manner of things may be revealed—the course of history past and future, or the secrets of the cosmos—but invariably the revelation focuses on a future divine judgment, which includes the judgment of the individual dead. The criteria for that judgment may vary from one apocalypse to another. In many (but not all) Jewish apocalypses, observance of the Mosaic law is crucially important. In Christian apocalypses, the criteria are supplied by the teaching and example of Christ.[4] What makes a vision apocalyptic, however, is not the specific teaching that it presents but that this teaching is said to be guaranteed by supernatural revelation and that it will be the criterion for the final judgment.[5]

The Dead Sea Scrolls include multiple copies of the apocalypses of Daniel and *1 Enoch*, but it does not appear that the sect that preserved these scrolls produced new apocalypses of its own. It had, however, an apocalyptic theology that was based on the certainty of divine revelation and of imminent judgment. This revelation was believed to be mediated by the Teacher of Righteousness and his successors. The teacher apparently superseded ancient apocalyptic visionaries such as Enoch and Daniel. Interestingly, Paul did not write apocalypses either, but his theology is also thoroughly apocalyptic. He too claimed to have divine revelation and believed that judgment was imminent.

In the case of the scrolls, the criterion for the judgment was supplied by the Torah of Moses, as interpreted by the sect. Most, if not all, Jews of the period revered the Mosaic law, but they often differed sharply from one another about its interpretation. The group that preserved the scrolls, however, was exceptional, insofar as it felt the need to separate itself from the rest of the people, because of the differences in interpretation. This is stated explicitly in 4QMMT C7, the text discussed by Martin Abegg in

---

in apocalyptic literature is also emphasized by C. Rowland, *The Open Heaven* (New York: Crossroad, 1982).

4. For a particularly clear example, see Matt. 25:31–46.

5. On apocalyptic rhetoric, see G. Carey and L. G. Bloomquist, eds., *Vision and Persuasion: Rhetorical Dimensions of Apocalyptic Discourse* (St. Louis: Chalice, 1999).

this volume. 4QMMT is an exceptionally interesting text, insofar as it seems to represent an attempt by sectarian leaders to reason with the authorities in Jerusalem. The attempt failed. Elsewhere in the scrolls we read that the Wicked Priest tried to kill the teacher because of the law, which he sent him.[6] But the rejection was hardly surprising. Even 4QMMT, which is exceptional among the scrolls in its attempt to address outsiders, does not offer reasons (such as exegetical arguments about the biblical laws) for the positions it affirms. It simply presents them as truth, known implicitly by revelation. The high priest and other leaders were not likely to be persuaded by these assertions, as they did not share the writer's belief that this interpretation of the Torah was inspired.

The community described in the scrolls, which is usually and plausibly identified as Essene, was clearly sectarian in the sense that it withdrew from the larger society and waited for God to vindicate it in the coming judgment. This community was relatively short-lived. It survived for less than two hundred years. The settlement at Qumran was apparently destroyed by the Roman army in 68 CE in the course of the Jewish revolt against Rome. But the Essene sect cannot be identified with only the settlement at Qumran. Philo (*Hypothetica* 11.1) and Josephus (*Jewish War* 2.124) tell us that the Essenes lived in many cities, and the sectarian rule books legislate for gatherings of as few as ten people (1QS 6.3, 6). It would be too simple, then, to attribute the demise of the Essenes to Roman military action. Rather, they died out because a theology based on the assertion of revelation, which could be only accepted or rejected, could not remain persuasive indefinitely. Incidentally, similar problems led to the demise of prophecy in the Old Testament. There, too, the confident assertion that one had "the word of the Lord" could not remain persuasive when prophets made claims that were often contradictory.[7]

The apocalypticism of Paul was not so extreme. While Paul's theology was fundamentally apocalyptic, he freely drew on the resources of Greek rhetoric and philosophy to render his preach-

6. 4Q171 4.8–9. See H. Eshel, "4QMMT and the History of the Hasmonean Period," in *Reading 4QMMT* (ed. J. Kampen and M. J. Bernstein; Atlanta: Society of Biblical Literature, 1996), 53–65.

7. See J. L. Crenshaw, *Prophetic Conflict* (Berlin: de Gruyter, 1971).

ing persuasive. He even entertains ideas that were indebted to philosophical ideas of natural theology (e.g., in Rom. 1). The success of Christianity as a missionary movement in the ancient world was due in no small part to the willingness of Christians to embrace elements of the pagan world. The use of Greek philosophy in the construction of Christian theology is an obvious case in point. Because of this, Christianity became enculturated in the Hellenistic world. For apocalyptic theologians such as Stanley Hauerwas, such enculturation was betrayal, but it was arguably the key to the survival and success of Christianity and to its extraordinary influence through the centuries.

I suggest then that the Dead Sea Scrolls do indeed hold salutary lessons for those who espouse an apocalyptic theology today. These lessons are cautionary ones. A theology that relies exclusively on apocalyptic assertion is not likely to be persuasive to many people for very long and runs the risk of self-marginalization and irrelevance. Apocalypticism is part of the Christian tradition and as such deserves respectful scrutiny and engagement. But it was never the only approach to Christian theology. A theology that is exclusively apocalyptic excludes too much of the tradition and is indeed appropriately labeled sectarian.

Index of Scripture and Other Ancient Writings

INDEX OF SUBJECTS AND NAMES